Over $1.2 Billion Won In 2 ½ Years!

WIN MORE GRANTS Like the Pros In 4 Steps

30 Top Secrets From 80 Grant Pros Reveal a Proven System That Virtually Guarantees Your Success!

By Phil Johncock, MA, MMs, GPC
93+% Success Rate

Introduction

So, you'd like to learn to write more winning grant proposals? You probably know that you're going to need to do a lot of hard work in order to learn everything there is to know about grants and grant proposal writing. You're probably already aware that you're going to need to spend at least two hours a day researching funders, and it's going to be very unpleasant and time-consuming, right?

Wrong! In fact, with the time-tested system that I'm going to show you today (30+ years in the making), you don't need to spend any time researching funders (Step 2) until you've first developed your idea into a fundable proposal (Step 1). This will eliminate 95% of your funder research time by focusing your precious time only on the best possible funding matches for your idea.

Students have told us that they enjoy reading real-life stories many that have come from my own personal experience or that of more than 80 experts.

In this book, you will learn only the most important techniques that we call "secrets". You will also discover a simple four step process that came from our research of what successful grant professionals say really works. These secrets will indeed make your life easier and help you win more grants in less time.

I look forward to sharing these best-kept 30 secrets with you and seeing your success rate soar! However, before I do, I'd like to share with you a short story in the next section about how a 57-year old man lost his job but then learned what's in this book to get a $75,000 grant. He even got hired to win more grants for a homeless shelter.

I hope you will enjoy this book!

Best of Success,

Phil Johncock
MA, MMs, GPC

P.S. In case you don't know much about me (Phil), I…

- Have taught thousands of students since 1993
- Designed the 1st grant proposal writing course on the Internet in 1997 (GrantWritingBasics.com)
- Created the 10-credit college grant proposal writing Certification Program in 2001
- Founded the Grant Professional Certification (GPC) Exam Prep Course Online in 2011 with a 100% success rate
- Have written over 60 winning grants with a 93%+ success rate
- Am Grant Professional Certified (GPC)

Testimonials

After losing his job, a friend shared an earlier version of this book. After getting a $75,000 grant, he got hired writing grants for a homeless shelter. Way to go!

Here's his story as told by my friend and grant professional, Doris Heroff...

"I wanted to tell you about one of the uses of your book that is very moving to me. There is this friend of mine who lost his job at the age of 57 with the church. He'd been a missionary and then as a journalist, writing a newsletter for pastors every month in the church group for almost 20 years.

He lost his job. I called him up when I heard about it. I said, 'With your skills as a journalist, you would probably be able to transfer your skills to the grants profession.'

After some conversations, I gave him your book. He agreed to come to volunteer at my agency. Within nine months, he was hired on the basis of having gotten a $75,000 grant from a foundation. He also did a bit of work for us on other small grants.

He was hired at a homeless shelter. So, he's doing mission work, and he's just doing it from another side. He's writing very well.

Thanks so much for your book!"

Doris Heroff
Grants Consultant
Minnesota

****

Here are more testimonials regarding the content on these pages...

I really liked the easy-to-follow and concise Secrets. I was given a lot of great information in a short amount of time.
~Ben Holland, Reno, NV

I like the way you provide the main points of grant proposal writing. I've read books as well as taken classes on grant proposal writing.
~Sharon Hughes-Foltin, IL

What I liked most about the secrets is that each secret discusses one aspect of grant proposal writing success. The secrets are short and to the point. I also like the summary at the end of the secrets where the major points are reviewed.
~Kristi Weeks, Las Vegas, NV

I am brand spanking new to the whole notion of grant proposal writing, and not a little intimidated and overwhelmed.
~Beverly Stanley, Brandon, FL

I liked that it was not overwhelming. It was easy to follow and has a good flow.
~Brianne Musselwhite, NY

I always thought that writing is so boring. I finally started to realize the art of writing.
~Lucy, Henderson, NV

It's straight to the point, short and simple.
~Steven Travis, Las Vegas, NV

The information is both practical and makes sense. It has to make sense to me. I also like it being in bites. I'm not overloaded with information.
~Bea Smith, Elgin, IL

Your ideas are helping me dream bigger. Your book is generating excitement and hope for potential grants. Your book is opening my eyes and widening the possibilities.
~Sonja Ellis, Las Vegas, NV

What I liked most about is that it's so Inspiring and is in connection with the Universal Laws. It leaves you with the feeling of wanting to learn more and more. I really didn't know what to expect since it was my first time looking into grant proposal writing. I thought that it might be dreadful but on the contrary I am really enjoying it! :)
~Rev. Diana Dolce, Staten Island, NY

I liked the five different observations of grant proposal writing experts. Learning this information truly helped me to begin thinking about writing a grant. I have no experience and knowledge of grant proposal writing and receiving this information was a great start for me.
~Stephanie, Las Vegas, NV

I enjoyed the fact that the secrets are short and to the point. They include suggestions and tips that I can incorporate right away in my grant proposal writing.
~Lisa Lucio, Mira Loma, CA

Unlike many educational programs, these secrets seem to apply to realistic situations.
~Jenifer, Las Vegas, NV

I liked the thought-provoking questions. This is my first time taking a grant proposal writing system so to have an organized way to think about the grant proposal writing process is beneficial.
~Teresa Pelham, Lancaster, SC

It has really changed my thinking. I was just thinking about money, but now my ideas are much bigger.
~Susan Kolar, Las Vegas, NV

It caused me to look beyond simply aspiring to write grants for others, which is fine, but to look into the dreams that I have and have always fostered. It made me believe that my dreams are possible, too.
~Betti Patterson, Chicago, IL

Everything is listed in steps. It makes grant proposal writing look a bit easier and less intimidating.
~Ellen Stark, Las Vegas, NV

I like that you can stay focused, be original, and be honest, straight forward, and most of all listen to others for their ideas and help. Believe in your project.
~Theresa Desmarais, Benson, AZ

What I like most is establishing the basics and setting up clear examples that anyone can do this and that a great idea is worth funding.
~Charlene Gibson, Las Vegas, NV

I liked that the process tied the grant proposal writing process to tapping into my own passion. Also mentioned was Social Artistry which I believe is critical at this time. The lessons instill a hopefulness in me that will allow me to make positive change.
~Christy Hirsch, Santa Rosa, CA

It is very common sense but thought-provoking.
~Jean Peyton, Las Vegas, NV

I liked the step-by-step format and the common-sense approach to what used to seem so daunting before I started.
~Ronald Harris, II, Attorney

I liked the specific instructions on how to get started on writing grants and that we are given additional information such as where to go to find funders...
~Dorothy Ratzlaff, Las Vegas, NV

I like the focus on passion and coming up with ideas from that passion. I like the short secrets with a big focus. That short secrets save me time in the day but have a big enough focus that I find I do a lot more thinking about one idea as opposed to trying to remember 50 ideas.
~Debbie Bloomquist, Cobb, CA

I liked the short and broken into sections that I could understand better.
~LeAnne Murphy, Las Vegas, NV

I learned informative, straight-forward, easy to understand information that will help me succeed in becoming a Grant Writer Certified. I wrote down questions of interest, key points, definitions, observations, and phrases of interest, all that were new to me. I found it interesting that something that I thought was taken for granted to be done by professionals only can be learned by me.
~Sandra Scott, Las Vegas, NV

What surprised me was how important my passion will be to my success.
~Didrik (Rik) Krogh, Las Vegas, NV

The secrets helped me better understand what is needed in order to be more successful at grant proposal writing. Ensuring the idea is well-developed and researching funders, customizing the proposal are key concepts which will help me in the future.
~Deborah, Wheeler-Williams, NV

I liked that each secret is easy to understand. Not knowing too much about Grant Proposal Writing (I was just told by a colleague I would be great at Grant Proposal Writing because of my current facilitation and documentation skill sets), I find it most useful to have each secret broken down into the simplest form.
~Eric Magallanes, Las Vegas, NV

Table of Contents

Step 3 – Customize Your Proposal **93**

Step 4 – Respond to the Decision **119**

Getting Started

Welcome!

My name is Phil Johncock. I am honored to share with you this important and timely book. Before we get to Secret 1, I would like to take a few, short moments to explain the best way for you to get started and get the most out of the system of 30 secrets and 4 steps.

In Secret 1, you will hear my story and how I used my first grant to create an ideal job for myself. In Secret 2, you'll expand your grant thinking. In Secret 3, you'll learn about the 4 basic steps of the grant proposal writing process and where they came from. These first three secrets set the foundation for the book.

Then, in Secrets 4-30, you'll explore the 4 steps of the grant proposal writing process used by pros:

Step 1 – Develop Your Idea Into Fundable Proposals

Step 2 – Research Funders

Step 3 – Customize Your Proposal

Step 4 – Respond to the Funder's Decision

Secrets 4-30 will be organized to deepen your understanding of the 4 steps of the grant proposal writing process used by many grant professionals.

The most important thing to remember is to learn and start applying the secrets right away. This will help you get grants more quickly.

The system on these pages has been time-tested over 31 years by thousands of students. They work.

Please keep in mind that some of the words in the "grant profession" might be new for you. "Grant writing" might be a new language for you, as it is for many people just starting out. If words are new, highlight or circle them. Keep in mind that it takes time for anyone to learn a new language. That's natural. Be patient with yourself. Give yourself plenty of time to simply read and learn.

In this book, you will also find checklists, worksheets and other forms that will make the grant proposal writing process easier for you. There will also be larger versions of checklists and worksheets that are too large to fit into this book's dimensions. To download larger versions (8 ½ x 11) that you can print and use, please visit **PhilJohncock.com/4-Steps**. These are great to come back to when you need them later. For example, you might come back to Secret 21 when you are preparing to contact a funder. Why? Because there you will find a comprehensive list of questions to ask funders before you even begin to write your proposal.

My biggest intention in creating this program for you is to make learning grant proposal writing faster, easier and more enjoyable. So, sit back and relax. Read and follow along. I look forward to sharing my story with you, as well as the 30 best-kept secrets from 80 experienced grant professionals.

These 30 secrets have changed my life dramatically and sky-rocketed my success rate to over 93%. I want them to change your life and help you be successful, too.

So, let's get started. And, I'll see you in Secret 1.

Secret 1 – Listen to the Experts

My Ideal Job!

One day in June 1988 - actually the very next day after graduating with my master's degree - I received a phone call from an administrator at the local community college. She was looking for someone to write a grant proposal for the college and asked me if I would be interested. I responded that while I was flattered to be asked, I had never written a grant proposal before; how could I possibly write a successful one?

"Don't worry," she replied. "The proposal is pretty straightforward. And if you need some help, just let me know."

I spent countless hours on that first grant. The guidelines were provided by the state department of education which outlined what was needed. However, it was my first grant, and I wanted to do the best I could. So I talked to experienced grant writers at the college, read old proposals that had been approved, and I asked a lot of questions-a lot of questions! I even watched a videotape on grant proposal writing-which put me to sleep after five minutes.

I probably spent more time on that first grant proposal than I did on the next ten combined!

Twelve years later, I had written 52 proposals, 48 which have been funded. That is an approval rate greater than 92 percent. Added together, these grants have secured over $6,300,000 for nonprofit organizations.

In 1993, due to popular demand, I was asked to teach a workshop on grant proposal writing at the community college. While I had had success in writing proposals, I didn't know if what worked for me would also work for others. Like most grant writers, I had had no formal training in grant proposal writing before I got started. So I started teaching intuitively, from personal experience.

I found myself explaining the process of grant proposal writing that seemed to work for me. And to complement my personal experience with a textbook, I chose a booklet touted as the "most widely used grant proposal writing format in the world."

As I spoke and shared my experiences, a model of the grant proposal writing process unfolded that I call the "idea match" model. Basically, this model starts with your ideas-your dreams. You begin with dreaming BIG, allowing your imagination to move beyond the limitations of what you think you know, perceive, and believe. Then you move your dreams out into the universe by expressing them on paper and including a budget.

IDEA MATCH

DEVELOP	CUSTOMIZE	RESEARCH
YOUR IDEA	YOUR PROPOSAL	FUNDERS
Step 1	Step 3	Step 2

Winning grants can sometimes be that simple. Dream BIG. Find your passion. Then, write down your dreams on paper, add a budget, and share your dreams with those around you. Often, that's all we need to do. Let go of the need to know right now how our ideas will get manifested. Share our ideas and our enthusiasm first. Magically, sometimes the funder for the dream suddenly shows up.

Recently, I told a class of teachers in arts education in California to practice stating their ideas clearly and concisely, in 30 seconds or less, to people around them. The next day at school, one of the teachers ran into the principal in the hallway.

After she shared her idea, the principal responded, "I just met with the PTA, and they're looking for a great idea to fund this year. I think your idea may be just what they're looking for." The art teacher never even had to write a proposal.

However, sometimes the universe-or more specifically a funding source, donor, or support service within our sphere of influence-is necessary to help us realize our dreams. Funders, whether private or public, want to be associated with winning ideas and with credible individuals and organizations. The idea match happens when funders' ideas of what they want to fund matches your idea of what you want to do.

Idea Match Story

I've got a great idea match story for you. Back in the spring of 1985, I was enrolled in a university course in career development. The final project for the class was to come up with our ideal job. We used inventories of our interests, analyses of our strengths, self-reflection exercises, and other career exploration activities to develop our ideas. Our ideal jobs could be ones that already existed, or we could be creative and make up new ones of our own.

At that time in my life, my dream was to create and direct a second-language learning program for adults. I had just moved to Reno, Nevada, after two years of living in central Mexico, teaching English as a second language (ESL) and learning Spanish.

I envisioned a model program that would provide innovative language learning opportunities, career-assisted instruction, support services (such as childcare, advisement, and tutoring), and creative ways of teaching and learning a second language. The program would incorporate my own experience of having taught ESL and having learned Spanish as an adult in Mexico. And of course, my ideal job would be to design and then coordinate the program.

I got an "A" on the assignment.

For the next several years I pursued this goal.

In the course of my project I had identified a master's degree as the education I needed for my ideal job. So I enrolled in and completed a master's degree program in teaching English. In graduate school I studied theories of second-language learning and teaching, while the ideal job lingered in the back of my mind as a 3-to-5-year goal for me to reach. I even kept an outline of my plan in my folder in my closet.

And then, exactly one day after I graduated with my master's degree, I received a call from the head of the ESL program at the community college, asking me to write a grant for the program. That first grant proposal was written to serve 250 newly legalized immigrants in a year. Amazingly, over 500 people showed up on our doorstep to take classes during the first week of registration.

So, I revised the grant several times-and asked for more funds. Since we had a waiting list of interested students in hand, the state department of education approved additional funds to serve the increased demand for classes. I wrote into the grant a position of program coordinator - my ideal job, remember?

Of course, the college had to open the position to all qualified applicants, and I had to apply for the job. However, I was confident that they would hire me. How could they refuse when I was so qualified, so enthusiastic about the project, and I even written a grant proposal?

Over a 5-year period we received more than $2.5 million in federal funds to serve more than 3,000 ESL students. We provided hundreds of classes in ESL, as well as classes in citizenship skills, life skills, computer literacy, earning a General Education Diploma (which is a GED, or high school equivalency), getting a driver's license, college preparation, and more.

The program also provided childcare, tutoring, career exploration, and other support services to help immigrants be successful. We rented a 100,000-square-foot space in the heart of the city to serve as our campus.

This first grant provided funding to hire over 30 teachers and tutors to teach over 400 60-hour courses. The program was recognized nationally as a model program.

Sharing this story of my first grant with my grant-writing students in 1993, when I first started teaching grant-writing, an interesting question popped into my head: "Had the final project for my career development class indeed manifested itself three years later?" In other words, had the ideal job magically appeared on the pages of the grant proposal that I was actually paid to write?

Hmmm. Then I wondered, "Perhaps that class project back in 1985 was basically a statement of my idea to the universe: 'Here ya' go, universe. Here's my dream, my ideal job. And here's the plan.'" Then I had to let go of how the idea would manifest itself. Once I got my master's degree-one of the prerequisites that I had set for the ideal job-the match happened. My idea, to create a language learning program, matched the funder's idea.

In this example, the funders-specifically, the federal government and the community college-wanted to fund a second-language learning and citizenship program for newly legalized immigrants: "O.K. Here you go. Here's the funding you need for your idea. To top it off, we'll pay you to write the grant, and you can include a coordinator position in the grant proposal."

I have many more idea match stories, many just as amazing as this one. Since 1993, I have shared these stories with hundreds of students, and they have shared theirs with me.

At one point, another thought popped into my mind: "Do other grant proposal writing experts adhere to the same idea match model that I do?"

It was hard to say.

I had interviewed and read student summaries of interviews with dozens of experienced grant writers and funders. There were dozens of ways to approach grant proposal writing and being successful.

I had checked out over 80 grant-writing and related books, and there were 80 distinct methodologies. I had surfed the Internet and read student summaries of countless web pages in grant proposal writing tips; there were as many slants as there were URLs.

In fact, curiosity about what the experts in the field of grant proposal writing think works best led me to design and write a second master's degree thesis on grant proposal writing.

Basically, I answered this question:

What do the grant proposal writing experts say really works?

This course is my humble attempt to answer this question. In it I share my own secrets as well as tips from the top grant proposal writing experts in the world. This course includes findings from my thesis, as well as my proven techniques that I've used in teaching and learning how to write a successful grant proposal.

So, what really is a grant?

And, what is grant proposal writing?

On the next secret, we'll find out what the grant proposal writing experts have to say.

Secret 2 – Expand Your Grant Thinking

What Is A Grant? What Is Grant Proposal Writing?

I'd like you to take a moment right now to think about the word 'grant'. What does it mean to you when you hear the word 'grant'?

What's the first thing that comes to mind? Is it 'money'? Is it 'government'? Is it 'funding'? What's the word or phrase that come to mind when you think about the word 'grant'?

According to the experts, 'grants' are "funds or money given by a funder to a grantee that doesn't have to be paid back." In other words,

- Funds are funding or money.

- A funder is a grant-maker or a donor.

- The grantee is the recipient, the agency or individual that receives the money.

A grant is a "gift that doesn't have to be paid back" like a loan does. It is any "public or private sector funding given for a specific purpose and time period as detailed in a specific application or proposal."

So, who are the grant-makers? Well, common grant-makers include foundations, corporations, federal and state government agencies, and even individual donors. I'll go into more detail about each of these in future Secrets.

Types of Recipient Agencies

Now, who gets the grants? Most recipients – or grantees – are tax-exempt with the IRS (501c3 designation) or non-profit organizations like schools and universities, state and local government agencies, churches, charities like the Boys and Girls Club, as well as businesses, even individuals.

You are about to see a comprehensive list of the typical agencies that typically receive grants. The question to ask yourself is: "Are any of these agencies ones that you currently work with or could work with in the future?"

The types of recipient agencies that typically get grant funds are …

Agencies: animal-specific agencies, arts/humanities organizations, churches/temples, civil rights groups, community improvement organizations, disease-specific health associations, educational institutions, environmental agencies, federated fund groups, government agencies, hospitals/medical care facilities, human service agencies, international organizations, media organizations, medical research institutes, mental health agencies, museums and historical societies, performing arts groups, professional societies and associations, public administration agencies, public and general health organizations, public policy institutions, recreation organizations, research institutes, science organizations, social science organizations, technical assistance centers, and youth development agencies.

Whew! There's a lot of agency types on that list. But, don't worry. It's just a long list of different types of agencies that have traditionally won grants in the past. So, if you were on the list, great. If you're not, that's O.K.

What Is Grant Proposal Writing?

While there is no agreement on which term most clearly describes the process of winning a grant - proposal writing, grant seeking, program development, even fundraising, or resource development, funding procurement, and grant proposal writing – but for the purpose of this course, the term "grant proposal writing" is the one that is most common and the one that we will use.

Grant writing refers to the "process, from start to finish, that results in a formal, written proposal being submitted to a funder." The funding is shifted then from the grant-maker to the grant-seeker.

Types of Support

What types of support do you need?

I'm going to give you another list. These are the most common types of support that you can get with a grant. Ask yourself, "Do I need any of these for my project?" Are you ready?

The types of support that recipient agencies typically get grant funds for are …

Support: Annual campaigns, building/renovation, capital campaigns, cause-related marketing, conferences/seminars, consulting services, continuing support, curriculum development, debt reduction, donated equipment, donated land, donated products, emergency funds, employee matching gifts, employee volunteer services, employee-related scholarships, endowments, equipment, exchange programs, fellowships, general/operating support, grants to individuals, in-kind gifts, internship funds, land acquisition, loaned talent, matching/challenge support, professorships, program development, program evaluation, program-related investments/loans, public relations services, publications, research, scholarships, scholarships for individuals, scholarships to institutions, seed money, sponsorships, student loans to individuals, technical assistance, and use of facilities

What do you do with these lists?

The reason I'm giving you these lists is for you to expand your mind and your thinking around grants.

These are considered "keywords" for you to keep in mind when you're researching grants on the Internet or you go to a free funding information center or Cooperating Collection in your state. The electronic databases for grants are organized by keywords for the type of recipient and type of support you need.

Areas of Interest

Grant databases may also ask you for your primary area(s) of interest. What things do you generally want to accomplish and do in the world? What problems do you want to solve?

Typically, grants can be categorized by fields of interest, using these keywords:

Interest: Agriculture/food, animals/wildlife, arts/humanities, civil rights, community development, crime/law enforcement, education, employment, environment, health care, health organizations, housing/shelter, human services, international affairs, international giving, medical research, mental health/crisis services, mutual aid societies, philanthropy/voluntarism, population groups, public affairs, recreation, religion, safety/disasters, science, social sciences and youth development.

Art and Science

Let's get back to the idea of winning more grants through smart "grant proposal writing." Smart grant proposal writing is 50% 'art', and it's 50% 'science'. It's 50% 'art' because we utilize 'art' combined with 'craft'. When I say 'art', I mean "personal, creative power." When I say 'craft', I mean some sort of "expertise in workmanship." By using your creativity and your technical writing skills, you are showing your 'art'.

When I say that smart grant proposal writing is 50% 'science', I mean that it uses "systematic knowledge of general rules." We obtain these rules and test them through some sort of scientific method. For example, we know from research that making a "pre-proposal contact" with a funder prior to submitting your proposal will increase - maybe double or even triple - your chances of being funded.

In the next Secret, I plan to share with you 5 general rules or part of the science of grant proposal writing that has emerged from my research of what 80 top grant proposal writing experts say really works.

Amazingly, though, even some of the best grant writers in the business can't claim a success rate greater than 50%. However, instead of reinventing the wheel yourself and having a low success rate, when you find a reliable grant proposal writing system that is based on both the art and science that has also been time-tested like this one has, you're more likely to increase your success rate dramatically. And, higher success rate means winning more grants.

Grant professionals are noteworthy social scientists. They research patterns, methods, and general truths and laws of what works. They share what works so that we all may benefit.

At the same time, grant professionals are remarkable social artists. They are flexible and creative artists, painting, sculpting, and dancing the world's problems in search of creative solutions in the fields of art, education, environment, health, human services, and social benefit.

In summary, grants are funds or money given by a funder to a grantee that doesn't have to be paid back. Grant writing is the process, from start to finish, that results in a written proposal being submitted to a funder or grant-maker.

This concludes Secret 2. In the next secret, we'll explore the science of grant proposal writing with 5 observations of the top grant proposal writing experts in the world.

Secret 3 – Summarize the Top Grant Proposal Writing Pros

To give you some context for the rest of the book…

I want to share with you 5 observations. In the course of doing my master's thesis and answering the question – What do the grant-writing experts say really works? - I researched top 80 books on grant proposal writing.

I analyzed the literature, and five themes emerged. I call these my five 'observations'.

Observation One: There's No One Single Best Method for Writing a Winning Grant Proposal

One of the first things I did in my thesis was to compare 12 different grant writers' different approaches to grant proposal writing. What steps do they follow in writing winning proposals? I noticed that each process was indeed different from the others. That is to say, each author describes a particular approach or process of grant proposal writing that works for him or her.

The variety of methods provides a richness of experience that we can all glean something from. I've enjoyed and learned much from each unique approach. I appreciate the incredible diversity.

On the other hand, as a grant professor, I realized that the variety can be overwhelming to beginning grant writers. Trying to put your arms around the vastness of information can be time-consuming and arduous.

Many grant writers – especially beginning ones - don't have the time to sift through so much information and make sense of it. And saving time for others and for myself - is important to me.

So, one of the intentions for this book is to make winning grants easier and save you time to do the things you most want to do.

Observation Two: A Proposal Should Be Customized To The Specifications Of The Potential Funder

One hundred percent of the authors – that means every single one of the 80 authors that I researched - agree on one point, namely, that all proposals should be customized, or tailored, to the specifications of the funder. This means that no matter what approach you use, you'll need to find out what guidelines and forms the funder has. Then, you follow the guidelines to a "t" and simply give them the information they want in the format that they wanted.

Failure to follow these requirements very likely means that your proposal may not even be considered, much less approved.

Proposal customization is like "customizing a resume." Let's say you're interested in getting a high-skilled job with an employer – perhaps let's call it Grant Writers, Inc. (GWI). Now, you could send GWI a resume that includes everything you've ever done – all of your education and experiences, your skills and abilities - everything plus the kitchen sink - in a 50-page, three pound monument to your life.

Now, would GWI be interested in you? Well, perhaps 'yes' because of your creativity and thoroughness. But most likely GWI's staff won't want to take the time to read your opus; in fact, they – like many reviewers -- allow, on average, less than five minutes to review each resume.

GWI's staff is interested in finding the best person for the job who meets the minimum qualifications, but they don't have lots of time to spend on the selection process.

They would need to hire a detective to investigate your 50-page manuscript to see if you indeed meet the qualifications of the job. And if the job itself requires brevity - ouch! You've already lost.

Let's say that, instead, you decide to send a generic 1-to-2-page resume to GWI, one that you also sent to 30 other companies this week. And, you started off your resume with "to whom it may concern." You're in the right page-number range, but this is called 'shot-gunning', and it doesn't get you any closer to the job at GWI. It often leaves a bad taste in the reviewer's mouth, for it appears that you're not interested enough in the company to even find out the name of the person to whom to send the resume.

Now, rather than sending in your complete biography or generic two-pager, you try a third approach. You instead research GWI and find out that they are looking for a certain type of person for the position - one who is concise, creative, organized, a team player, with accounting experience preferred. Let's start there. You begin to get a feel for GWI, and you start to see it's a company you would like to work for. You know that you've got a lot to contribute to any job, so you want to be selective.

Supposing that you like the potential fit with GWI. You can then take some time to tailor the description of your education and your work experiences so that they relate to what GWI is most interested in, its specifications. You write this up in a 2-page, customized resume.

The chances of getting an interview have increased significantly - as has the likelihood that you would win the job.

Like resumes customized to a potential employer, a winning grant proposal should be likewise tailored to the potential funder's specifications.

"So, where do you find the funder specifications?" you may ask.

Well, where do you find employer specifications? Where do they post publicly that there is a job available?

- Usually they're available publicly somewhere in print.

- Once in a while, you have to ask them.

- Occasionally, they don't exist at all.

It's the same with funders. In Step 2 - Researching Funders - you'll find specific information that will help you find out where funders make their specifications public, how to best analyze them, how to get the guidelines and forms, and how to determine -- in the least amount of time possible -- what the funders are looking for in a winning proposal.

Before we move on to Observations 3, 4 and 5, I'd like to review Observations 1 and 2. Observation 1 is "There's no single best method for writing a grant." Observation 2 is "A proposal should be customized to the specifications of the potential funder."

So, let's move on to Observation Three.

Observation Three: Develop Your Idea First

Most of the winning authors I researched – 83% of them - agree that the first step in the grant proposal writing process is to develop the idea which you are seeking money for - before you attempt to identify potential funders. There are five reasons they give for doing this:

Reason 1 - First, developing your idea first, even if on a small scale, encourages you to adequately assess the needs of the population or people you plan to serve. Or, you can assess the needs of the nonprofit agency that you're working with or the community in which you plan to implement your idea. By assessing needs, you ensure that what you propose includes input from others who may benefit. Then, they begin to accept ownership of the solution.

Reason 2 - Developing your idea first can also ensure that you have identified any gaps in your agency's ability to accomplish its overall mission. Once gaps have been identified, the agency can determine how and where to best direct its current available resources and then proactively go after funding and grants to respond to its calling, its mission.

Reason 3 - Developing your idea initially also allows for a wider range of potential funders to be considered and identified. When you are clear on what you specifically need - such as computers, fencing, papers and pencils, books, a new building, or just money - it comes easier to identify potential funders when you know what you want.

Reason 4 - Developing your idea before anything else primes the dream-making pump, as in the story of my first grant. When I developed the plan for my ideal job, I gave thought to what I wanted. The result was a plan - like a business plan - that included pieces of the puzzle that needed to fall into place for my dream to come true.

Developing your idea into a fundable plan ensures that all the major pieces of the puzzle are included. Then, once you know what format the funder requires, it's a piece of cake to pick and choose from what you've already come up with, even cut and paste which you've already written into a real proposal. Getting clear about what it is you really want, cultivating and kneading your ideas thoroughly, and developing the key components of what most funders are looking for will serve you later and save you time in the long run.

Reason 5 – And, this may actually surprise you. Letting go of 'how' you think your dream should come true. For me, developing ideas first makes dream-making come alive - then the unfoldment becomes magical. Letting go of how the idea will manifest itself, if nothing else, leads to an interesting story!

As we just saw in Observation 3, you can start by developing your idea first. Observation 4 says that a smaller minority of the experts actually start by searching for funders first.

Observation Four: Or, Start With Searching For Funders

A few of the authors - 17% in fact - identify funding sources first. And, this works well, as well. That is, you can begin to find potential funding sources that are interested in giving in your area of concern - say, education, health or the environment - and they're interested in giving in your geographic area.

When you find one that you or your agency is eligible for, you apply. Having guidelines from the funders up front can even help you develop your ideas further. You can begin to customize your idea right away, filling in the information that is needed to present your project at its best in the eyes of the funder.

Now, I've facilitated a lot of meetings to brainstorm ideas once we've learned that the money has become available for which an agency is eligible to apply. We discuss how the agency and the group can creatively develop an idea in order to be competitive in getting the money that's available, while making sure that we address the mission of our agency.

Observation Five: There Are Four Basic Steps To Grant Proposal Writing

As I analyzed the 12 grant proposal writing approaches,4 primary steps appeared that most winning grant writers seem to follow. Here are the 4 steps:

Step 1 - Develop your idea.

Step 2 - Research potential funders (whose ideas match yours).

Step 3 - Customize your proposal (to match the funder's specification).

Step 4 - Respond to the funder's decision.

Later, I took this four-step process, and I classroom-tested it with hundreds of students. I found that presenting the process in these four simple steps makes teaching and learning the art of grant proposal writing easy, while giving students a common foundation to build their skills and experiences on.

If I had had a model like this to help me when I first started, it would have saved me hundreds of hours, as well as motivated me to dream and imagine even greater things. Moreover, the tips from experienced grant writers can easily be categorized under these four steps.

In review, Observation Three said to "Develop your idea, first." Observation Four is that "You can start with searching for funders first." And, Observation Five says "There are 4 basic steps to grant proposal writing":

1. Develop your idea.
2. Research funders.
3. Customize your proposal.
4. Respond to the funder's decision.

Next, we will learn more about Step 1 – Develop Your Idea in Secrets 4 through 13. In Secret 4, you'll learn about the power of dreaming big.

STEP 1
DEVELOP YOUR IDEA

Secret 4 - Dream Big

In a study of top grant proposal writing experts and in my thesis, 83% of them agreed that the first step in writing a grant is to develop the idea for which you are seeking money.

The process of developing your idea is exciting. It's like planting idea seedlings and watching their growth as they move into fully grown fundable proposals. I call the process "Dreaming BIG."

Why is it important to dream big?

Goethe once said, "Whatever you can do or dream you can, begin it. Boldness has genius, power, and magic in it."

Psychology tells us that self-limiting thoughts and beliefs keep us from developing our full human potential. The Law of Attraction says that bad feelings, negative thoughts, and focusing on what we don't want result in attracting the opposite of what we really want.

Let's take a look at a man who had a BIG dream that has affected us all. His name is President George W. Bush. One of his slogans was "leave no child behind." Whether you agree with the program or not, you have to agree that the dream was indeed a big one … that every child in the U.S. is important, even though some children are less successful in education than others.

Likewise, every person's dreams and ideas are important, even though some are less successful in manifesting their dreams than others. Perhaps the slogan of this secret should be "leave no dream behind."

What if you believed your ideas and dreams were not only important, but absolutely necessary for the betterment of our planet. Keep in mind that funders – namely, foundations, corporations, government agencies and individual donors – actually give over $300 billion every year in grant funding to somebody's dreams and ideas. They have to!

So, if someone's dreams and projects have to get funded, why not yours?

There is a saying, "IF NOT YOU, WHO? IF NOT NOW, WHEN?"

I bet you have an idea right now, a potential for causing change or creating something that didn't exist before. Perhaps there's a big problem like world hunger you would like to help solve. Or, you have invented something that could help communities lower energy costs.

There may simply be a compelling personal need that is driving you from within or a need in your community that is driving you from without. You may be looking at a need in the community that is going unmet and there must be a way to meet that need.

_____
Your Idea

You may want to further your career or volunteer after retiring to pursue a project that will aid your community or church.

Everyone I know has ideas for projects, solving problems, or fulfilling unmet needs. You may have a very clear idea right now of what you want to get a grant for. You're a teacher and you want travel funds to attend a conference on renewable energy sources on the other side of the country. You're a mother who wants to insulate the walls in the drafty room in your day care center. (In fact, my mother got a grant for just that!)

You're an entrepreneur, and you want to develop new ways to bring jobs into your community using the power of the Internet and social media like Facebook, Twitter and You Tube. You want to help people on welfare and unemployment, especially single parents, while putting your own company on the map at the same time.

You are a film maker who wants to shoot a documentary about successes of foster children or about an AIDS education project whose story you are so compelled to help tell. Or, you are someone who hasn't come up with a project yet, but you feel it's time to give back or maybe pay it forward.

_____
Another Idea

Gandhi said, "The difference between what we're doing and what we're capable of doing would solve most of the world's problems."

So, I have two questions for you:

1. If you had unlimited funds, what big dream would you pursue?

_____

_____

2. If funding were not an issue, what big problems would you like to solve?

_____

_____

So that we get the ball rolling faster, I invite you to share you answers to these two questions with at least two other people in the next 24 to 48 hours.

Person 1:_____   Date:_____

Person 2:_____   Date:_____

In review, Step 1 of the grant proposal writing process is to Develop Your Idea into a fundable proposal. Today's Secret is to start by Dreaming BIG.

In Secret 5, we'll explore how to tap your inner passion to keep your dream going.

Secret 5 – Tap Into Your Passion

I am assuming that you have a big dream or project that you would like to see manifested in the world. If you don't, just act as if you do.

In this secret, you will learn why it's important to tap into your passion. It's an unlimited supply of energy that will fuel your idea or project forward.

I'm going to invite you to do something scary. Are you ready?

I'm going to ask you to share your excitement about your idea and project with 3 other people. Not, quite yet. But, soon enough.

I want you to brainstorm with me for a moment in this Secret one of your biggest dreams. I want you to stretch your imagination beyond the realm of the likely and familiar.

I'd like you to choose in this moment just one - one idea, or one problem, or one population group that would like to work with. You only need one. I want you to call this one idea, this one problem, this one population group … your "dream".

Let me explain what I mean …

Your idea could be anything innovative that you feel excited to bring out into the world. It could be an invention or a unique discovery.

Or, you could choose your problem, which could be any social need that is grabbing your attention these days. It could be foreclosures, friends out of work, a family whose sudden medical bills just bankrupted them.

Or, you could choose a special population group - any special group that you are drawn to work with. Here are some for you to choose from. It could be working with the aging, alcohol and drug abusers, children and youth, crime or even with abused victims - how about the disabled, economically disadvantaged, homeless, immigrants and refugees, men and boys, military and veterans, minorities, offenders and ex-offenders, people with AIDS, single parents, women and girls.

Choose an idea or problem or population that first comes to mind. You don't need all three, just one. Take a moment; write down that one idea, problem or population. That's the first thing to do.

_____
Your Idea, Problem or Population

If you can't find one of these, then pause and re-read this secret. This is important. I want you to write down something: an idea, problem or population group that you would like to work with.

Now, let me ask you another question, "Do you believe that you have access right now, in this moment, to a limitless energy source that could fuel you forward indefinitely towards getting what you need – whether it be funding, donations, resources, people – whatever it is you need to realize your dream?"

Would you like to know what that free energy source is?

The answer is (drum roll) … your passion. It's your enthusiasm for doing what you really love to do. It's the way you refresh and rejuvenate yourself from inside out. It's the way you keep going towards manifesting your dreams, even when those around you are naysayers or trying to pooh-pooh your ideas.

Joseph Campbell once said, "*If you follow your bliss, you put yourself on a kind of track that has been there all the while, waiting for you, and the life that you ought to be living is the one you are living. Wherever you are - if you are following your bliss, you are enjoying that refreshment, that life within you, all the time.*"

To help you access that passion inside – that passion for your idea to address the problem or work with a population group - let me ask you one other question:

"What 'excites you most' about your idea or the problem or the population you would like to work with?"

I want you to write that down. I want you to write down what it is that excites you most about your idea.

_____

_____

_____

_____

_____

Now, I'd like you to share your answer to this question with at least 3 people in the next 8 hours.

Person 1:_____   Time:_____

Person 2:_____   Time:_____

Person 3:_____   Time:_____

As you open up to what motivates and excites you about your ideas, problems and people, you tap into an inner strength and wealth of energy that will sustain you even through the tough times …

- When others think you're crazy,

- When you're stressed and overwhelmed,

- When deadlines draw near, and

- When other priorities and commitments vie for your attention.

Tap your passion, and you'll move through challenging times like they're butter. And, you stay on course to make your dreams come true.

In review, come up with an idea, problem or population group you would like to work with. Then, tell at least 3 people what excites you most about that idea, problem or population group.

This concludes Secret 5. In the next secret, you'll learn 2 ways to be original and attract funders.

Secret 6 – 2 Ways To Be Original & Attract Funders

Grant funding sources like Foundations, Corporations, Government Agencies and even Individual Donors prefer projects that are "original".

In this secret, you will learn how to make your proposal more attractive to funders by using the power of 'originality'.

As you might guess, a truly original idea will stir interest and attract attention. Here are two proven ways to attract funder attention with your original ideas:

1. Be first – Find out some methodology, some approach or system in your field that has been proven successful elsewhere in the country, but has never been tried in your geographic area. The early bird does indeed get the worm. By being the earliest program, you will be perceived as being novel, forward-thinking, progressive.

    Funders in your geographic area will be impressed that you are the first, even though you know that you're not. It's your secret! You're smart, building on the successes of others and initiating first. You'll beat the competition to the punch.

    Here is proven way number 2:

2. Be new and fresh – Some of the biggest social problems in the world – poverty, hunger, educational disadvantages – have been around forever. Many of the same old problems could be viewed as stale and outdated when a fresh, new approach is presented.

    For example, I have a friend who brings his own creative genius in performing arts to social problems like death and dying, at-risk high school students and the foster care system. Instead of using traditional methods, he uses dancing, singing, comic books - all that create extraordinary results. Funders – even conservative ones like the Department of Justice – absolutely love him and his programs!

    Think of how your project could bring something totally new and fresh to existing problems. Tap into your beginner's mind to explore ways your program could be unique, innovative, novel, inventive, creative, and unusual.

In review, if you want your project to be more attractive to funders, use two proven ways to be original. First, be first. And, second, be new and fresh.

In the next secret, we'll look at how to make your ideas more fundable by looking at how to make them more timely.

Secret 7 – Timely Ideas That Attract Funders

In this Secret, you will learn how to make your proposal more timely.

You see, timely ideas attract funders. Let me explain …

Times change. Perceptions change. This is true in the social and political arenas as well as in the arts and sciences. Prior to 9-11, security in the U.S. was important, but not as timely and critical as it is today. A new office for Homeland Security was even created after 9-11, and funding was allocated for homeland security. In fact, a lot of new grant funding is being pumped into homeland security.

Why? Because it is 'timely'.

Timing is everything in politics. For example, when a Republican is in the Presidency or in control of Congress, less government and taxes is the rally call.

Several year's ago, there was a huge political opening made in the world of non-profits. Prior to that time, churches were not eligible to receive grants from the Federal government. That all changed when it was passed into law that faith-based organizations and initiatives were now eligible for government grants. This shift was huge! The separation between church and state that existed before is suddenly blurred. In one swoop of the pen, over 500,000 religious organizations in the U.S. were suddenly eligible for grant funding, where before they weren't. For grant writers looking for a niche market, try churches.

What's important to our communities also changes. Our attitudes and ideas about what's important comes and goes. For example, in 2009, the legislative branch of our government passed the American Recovery and Reinvestment Act, which allocated over $400 billion in extra grant funding – called the Stimulus Package - to kick start the economy, or at least try to.

Likewise, at times of high gas prices, alternative fuels and sources of energy becomes important. In his first State-Of-The-Union Address, President George W. Bush pledged a billion dollars in grants to research biodiesel technology. Timing is indeed everything.

And, timely ideas are 'opportunistic'. A well-timed curve ball from a pitcher catches the hitter off guard and leads to an out and one step closer to a victory. A well-timed speech like that of a Winston Churchill can solidify the entire nation and activate a call to action within its citizens. Your idea, if strategically placed, could be the perfect timed solution.

Keep in mind that funders, too, change in their areas of interest to deal with the perceived social problems and issues of the future. For example, a funder might change its funding priorities from more global to local. It may have addressed financial concerns in the international community before. But, now they're focusing on helping nonprofits in ways that help ensure the charity's very survival. Five years ago, maybe this funder provided seed money and frowned upon funding operating expenses. But, that may have changed today.

Here are three questions to ask in order to make your idea more timely:

1. What is particularly timely about your idea?

2. What is particularly timely in the social, political, education, science, arts, humanities or other areas?

3. What is "not" particularly timely about your idea?

In review, timely ideas attract funders. Times change. Perceptions change. And, our ideas and attitudes about what is important come and go. Your timely ideas, if strategically placed, can be the perfect timed solution that attracts funding.

The three questions to ask are: 1) What is timely about your idea? 2) What is particularly timely in the social, political, education, science, arts, humanities or other areas? 3) What is 'not' particularly timely about your idea?

This concludes Secret 7. In the next Secret, we'll discover 3 ways to solve problems and attract funders.

Secret 8 – 3 Top Ways to Solve Problems & Attract Funders

Grant funding sources like Foundations, Corporations, Government Agencies and even Individual Donors prefer projects that are original, timely and "provide solutions to problems." To increase your chances of getting funded, make sure your proposal is original, timely and provide solutions to problems. Today, in Secret 8, you will learn how to make your proposal more attractive to funders by providing solutions to problems.

Have you ever noticed that certain problems always seem to be with us, like hunger, poverty, violence, pollution, injustice, suppression of human rights, discrimination, crime? These are issues that tug on the very fabric of society and our communities. They test our resolve. They often include conflicts among the interests of community members, as well as clashes of values. They lie beyond the control of any one individual.

Funding sources or funders have missions that frequently address the larger social problems that are not being addressed by individuals or other means, such as capitalism. If someone could figure out how to profit by ending big problems like pollution or poverty, then for-profit business could step in. Then, there would be less need for charitable organizations to address the unmet needs. However, this is unlikely to happen in our lifetimes.

As a grant writer, you are a noteworthy social artist who use your creative ingenuity and your technical craftsmanship to paint, sculpt and dance the world's problems in search of creative solutions. Technically, to be successful and save time, I've learned over the years that it's most helpful to have several different grant proposal writing templates to use to illustrate the problems you wish to solve, as well as the methodology you wish to use in solving them.

So, I recommend one template for corporate and foundation letter proposals that are 1-4 pages in length. I recommend a second template for larger government grants. Regardless of the templates you use, to increase your chances of being funded, every template must have the 3 basic problem-solving components that any grant proposal has to have:

1. Your problem statement

2. Your solution and method

3. Your evaluation

   I'll explain each of these in more detail. Ready?

1. Your Problem Statement – Your problem statement is the most critical part of your proposal. Since most funders are interested in funding programs in specific states or geographic areas, you need to take the problem that exists in your community and relate it to similar situations that exist in other communities. This shows the broader implications of your problem. You can do this by using statistical evidence from a national, state and local level, as well as statements from authorities in your field.

   Where do you find statistics? I suggest you become friends with your nearest librarian and the person nearest you who's familiar with the U.S. Census. Also, check your professional association in your area of interest for facts, statistics and quotes from authorities in your area. These help illustrate the problem.

2. Your Solution and Method – To solve any problem, you need a method or a tool. Once you have described a problem adequately, the next step is to spell out *how* you will solve the problem. The way you show how is by listing the activities, procedures, tasks or strategies you propose. I prefer to use what is called, "Activity Timeline."

A C T I V I T Y   T I M E L I N E

ACTIVITY	11/98	12/98	1/99	2/99	3/99	4/99	5/99	6/99	7/99	8/99	9/99	10/99	11/99	12/99
Secure a web address and link current web-page	X													
Secure electronic mailing list and regular mailing list for individuals and agencies	X	X												
Design and print flyers	X	X												
E-mail electronic flyer			X											
Mail three–fold flyer			X											
Purchase qeuipment for interviews/audio clips	X													
Conduct, record, and edit interviews/audio clips			X	X	X	X	X	X						
Hire web consultant to put audio clips and transcripted versions on the website							X	X						
Evaluate outcomes and processes														X

   The basic requirements of your method are clarity and justification. This means that it's important to list your activities you need to solve the problem and describe as clearly as possible the tasks you plan to do.

3. Your Evaluation – It's not enough to state that there is a problem and a solution. You have to show how you plan to measure your progress and

success in solving the problem. In other words, you are asked upfront to show how you will be accountable once you spend the grant money. To do this, include the activities that you will do, the staff you will hire, the deadlines for completing your activities. You will be asked to use acceptable and reliable measurements – like test scores – to show improvement of your clients.

I'm going to give you 3 questions to ask yourself to make sure that your idea solves a problem:

1. What big problem does your idea attempt to solve?

    _____

2. What activities do you need to do to solve the problem?

    _____

3. What evaluation tools you will you use to measure your success?

    _____

In review, funders like foundations, corporations, government agencies and individual donors want to address big social problems that are not being solved by for-profit businesses. You can increase your chances of being funded when you include the 3 basic problem-solving components in every grant proposal you write:

1. Your problem statement

2. Your solution and method

3. Your evaluation

This concludes Secret 8. In the next secret, we'll discover 3 ways to make your ideas more attractive to funders by making them more compelling.

Secret 9 – 3 Aspects of Compelling Ideas That Attract Funders

The most compelling ideas are the ones that influence the reviewers and leave a lasting impression. They hold the attention of the reader like a compelling movie about human relations keeps the audience glued to their seats. They move us emotionally and necessitate action.

In this Secret, you will learn how to make your proposal more "compelling". And, compelling ideas attract funders.

Here are 3 aspects of compelling ideas:

1. Compelling Ideas Hold People's Attention

2. Compelling Ideas Move Us Emotionally

3. Compelling Ideas Necessitate Action

Let's take a look at each of these aspects.

Aspect 1 - Compelling Ideas Hold People's Attention

Have you ever watched a compelling movie about human relationships that engaged you right from the start and kept you interested for the entire 2 hours? One of these movies for me was *Dances with Wolves*. From the beginning, I found myself leaning forward. I didn't sit back until the lights came on over 3 hours later, and I had to leave.

Likewise, if your idea is compelling, it will hold the reader's attention right from the start.

- Start with a creative, descriptive title. I like to use acronyms, like Project R.I.C.O. – RICO stands for *Raising Income through Career Opportunities*. Here's another title: W.I.N. Project or the W.I.N. Project - *Welcoming Immigrants to Nevada*.

- Then, weave a common thread throughout the entire proposal. For me, the thread is 1-2 specific outcomes that align with the funder's interests, like using 'increase' or 'decrease'. For example, a common thread could be "to increase graduation rates" or "to decrease recidivism." This point becomes the "central selling proposition" that matches the funder's idea of what they would like to fund. In other words, if the funder is interested in increasing graduation rates, and you've included this as a common thread throughout your entire proposal, there's a match, and you'll get funded.

Aspect 2 - Compelling Ideas Move Us Emotionally

The Make a Wish Foundation has a compelling idea. What can be more rewarding than fulfilling wishes of a dying child. You can't help but be moved. When we're moved, we open our wallets and purses.

Aspect 3 - Compelling Ideas Necessitate Action

I wrote my first grant for $125,000 to educate 250 newly legalized immigrants. I wanted to ask for more, but my boss said it would be better to start small, conservatively. This didn't last long. In the first week of registration over 550 people showed up on our doorsteps.

I got this great idea. What if we served all 550 people with the money we were allocated. Everyone would get served, but we would run out of money in less than half the time - in this case, 6 months. I knew that this would force some sort of action. We have to close our doors – and here's the crux – unless we received more money.

With this idea in mind, I approached the State Department of Education. It didn't take much convincing, though, to get them to take the appropriate steps to secure more funding.

- Nothing sells better than success.

- Under-promise and over-deliver.

- When your idea is compelling, it compels funders to take action. Everyone wants to be on the side of a winner!

Make your ideas forceful (but not overbearing), convincing, persuasive, undeniable, and gripping – and then see what happens.

I'm going to give you 3 questions to ask yourself to make your idea more compelling:

1. What about your idea grabs people's attention?

_____

_____

Here's one idea for how you can answer this question. Tell your colleagues or friends about your idea. Ask them to tell you what grabbed their attention the most when you shared your idea.

2. What about your idea moves people emotionally?

_____

_____

3. How can you explain your idea in such a way that it compels the funder to take action?

_____

_____

In review, the 3 aspects of compelling ideas are …

1. Compelling Ideas Hold People's Attention

2. Compelling Ideas Move Us Emotionally

3. Compelling Ideas Necessitate Action

This concludes Secret 9. In the next Secret, we'll discuss how to include a sustainability plan that will show the funder how your project will continue after the funding you receive initially is gone.

Secret 10 – 21 Strategies for a Killer Sustainability Plan

You may have heard of the term "seed money." Basically, it refers to how funders prefer to fund a project the first time, plant the seeds for future growth. The funder expects that you will be able to sustain the program once it's started.

Why? Donors are not interested in adopting a project indefinitely.

Funders want insurance that the project they fund – or the benefits that it generates – will endure over time.

Ask yourself 2 questions …

1. What kind of assurance can you give that the idea or project you're proposing will endure over time?

2. What strategies can you implement that will increase chances that what you start will be sustained and maintained over time?

The Sustainability Plan is the weakest part of most grant proposals. In this secret, you will learn 21 strategies to create a sustainability plan that will leave your competitors in the dust.

I learned the "sustainability" lesson the hard way. Here's my story …

In 1993, the $2.5 million in federal grant funding ended. I didn't realize until it was too late that the Fed's were serious about only giving grants for five years.

Sadly, we had no sustainability plan in place.

I had to let go of 25 teachers and tell 3,000 students – who were newly legalized immigrants – that they no longer had classes. We were able to sustain some classes on a fee-for-service basis. However, the heart of the program died with the funding. I was devastated.

I hadn't realized until it was too late that getting grant "seed money" is a blessing AND a curse. On the one hand, the money can create many great projects and do great things. On the other hand, agencies are responsible for coming up with their own ways to sustain their efforts after they've started.

21 Sustainability Strategies

Here are 21 "proven" strategies to choose from for your sustainability plan …

1. Apply for other grants from other sources. But, keep in mind that other funders may not be interested in keeping the program going either.

2. Let the organization itself absorb future funding responsibilities (that is, if the agency is large enough). This happened in the case of a Single Parent – Displaced Homemaker program at the local college. The President and college administration found ways to use more secure state funding combined with various federal and state grants to keep the program going, but only after it had proven itself.

3. Use fee-for-service. Charge the clients a portion of the cost as tuition or fee. When my first grant funding dried up, we convinced the county and city to fund a portion of the cost of the classes. We charged the students the rest. This reduced students' costs. (A variation of this would be to use a "sliding scale.")

4. Use sponsorships or 3rd party subsidies. For example, a large summer camp for handicapped children gets corporations or individual donors to "sponsor" a kid for the summer. Programs like "adopt-a-hungry kid" or "adopt-an-orphan" or even "adopt-a-whale" are great sponsorship programs.

5. Start a for-profit enterprise. Our local disabled adults do projects like running a clothing store, putting labels on envelopes for future mailings or even help with horticulture projects. This idea literally puts clients to work.

6. Do annual fundraisers. Select a "high return on investment" fundraiser that you can do on an annual basis, like a golf tournament, celebrity event, concert, raffle, dinner, or roast.

7. Develop recurring revenue options, like membership sites. For example, create a "membership website" that takes what your agency does and shares something every month with your members. One local nonprofit records interviews with visiting monks and scholars and provides these as MP3's for 'paid' members to download from the website.

8. Create an endowment campaign. Most large charities have caught on that one of the best ways to sustain programs is by creating an endowment fund. Basically, an endowment fund invests the money received and spends a percentage – like 5% or so - every year from the interest made of

the investment of its assets. This is how many foundations work. You're able to spend the interest from investing your assets each year without touching the principal.

9. Create a Planned Giving program. These may be called "wills" or "bequests," gifts that are given when a person transitions or dies. According to Giving USA, in 2008, over $22.66 Billion was given in bequests.

10. Create a Development office (or expand the one you have). In addition to grants, a Development office can coordinate Planned Giving, an endowment campaign, and other forms of fundraising.

11. Create a unique campaign. Capital campaigns are popular initiatives to pool resources and pull people together to focus on raising money to build a building. You can also create a campaign for almost anything, like a class trip, Christmas gifts for needy children, or food drive for the hungry.

12. Create a scholarship office. Pool your efforts to assist students or clients in finding grants and loans to pay for their own education or programs. Consolidate everything in a one-stop location. The university from which I received my first Bachelors degree says that at least 86% of its students are receiving scholarships. I love how the students there are involved in helping other students find their own scholarships.

13. Create a special tax initiative. Contact your U.S. or state Senator or Representative who is sympathetic to your project. Brainstorm with the person how to get state funding or start a tax initiative. One community college and high school in Florida combined their efforts along with state representatives to secure $1 million in a "planning grant" to build a new tech center that could be shared by high school students during the day and college students at night and weekends.

14. Do what you do best. Delegate the rest. Perhaps some of the aspects of your program could be picked up by another organization. For example, your intake could be picked up by an agency that specializes in that. Your marketing could be absorbed by another agency who has the experience to do that. Then, you specialize in what you do best.

15. Invite Facebook donations. This is especially helpful when someone on your board or someone in your organization is having a birthday. One way to celebrate the birthday is by promoting and giving to your cause online. Money can be raised directly from your Facebook page.

16. Let other businesses raise money for you. The local grocery chain features a different nonprofit every month. A certain percentage of all purchases on a certain day goes to the nonprofit. I see this a lot in the fall when businesses donate office supplies and needed items to children going back to school, based on the purchases that you make.

17. Engage clients in your campaign. Empower your clients to get involved in Pay It Forward or some sort of campaign that gets them interested in helping out with the fundraising and giving back. You can look at alumni associations for colleges and universities for good example of this. You can focus on what clients do "after" they receive services. Or, you can also focus on what they can do "during" the time when they are receiving services. This is great because they have a vested interest in keeping the funding coming and the program going.

18. Create and sell products online. The Food for Everyone Foundation has written some great books on organic gardening. These are available online with proceeds going to the Foundation. So, create products – like eBooks, MP3's, Special Reports – using your nonprofit's expertise.

19. Train others (online). One of my clients, Rogue Retreat, created Hope University as a platform to teach other communities what they have learned around working with the homeless. Their vision is to give the homeless "hope". First, they started with 25 people attending a Community Village Creation 101 five-week teleconference course that was repurposed into a five-part audio course with audio recordings and handouts. Second, they offered a Winter Shelters 101 3-week teleconference course. Moving forward, they have other courses being planned. For examples, visit this website URL:

RogueRetreat.com/Hope-University

20. Become an affiliate. Align yourself and your agency with a product or service in your area. Then, when you refer someone, your agency receives a commission. It's important that this be part of your mission, though, and that you check with your accountant. In the worst case scenario, the revenue could be 'taxed' and not 'tax-exempt' if it's not related to your mission.

21. Apply for membership in federal fundraising initiatives. For example, apply to the United Way for ongoing funding from corporate donations.

In review, funders like to give grants in the form of "seed money." Funders want insurance that the project they fund – or the benefits it generates – will endure over time. So, ask yourself two questions:

Question 1 - What kind of assurance can you give that the idea or project you're proposing will endure over time?

_____

_____

Question 2 - What strategies can you implement that will increase chances that what you start will be sustained and maintained over time?

_____

_____

Use the 21 proven strategies to create your own Sustainability Plan.

This concludes Secret 10. In the next secret, we'll talk about having your 15-second elevator pitch ready in case you run into a potential donor.

Secret 11 – Have Your 15-Second Elevator Pitch Ready

You never know when you're going to run into a person who is a potential donor for your project. If not, perhaps she knows someone who could be a potential donor. Way back in Secret 1, I told you the story of an arts teacher in California who ran into the principal in the hallway the day after she learned this secret.

She shared her elevator pitch – which was to have her students decorate the dilapidated tables in the cafeteria as an art project. All she needed was $2,000.

The principal had just met with the PTA, and they were looking for a $2,000 project to fund. The principal thought her idea was a perfect fit. The art teacher never even had to write a proposal.

The important thing to remember is to be ready for the next opportunity to share your idea. What's key, though, is that you need to make it short and get to the point.

So, imagine that you happened to get on an elevator and there was a potential donor – like Bill Gates or Oprah Winfrey. You have 15 seconds – to grab their attention, share your enthusiasm and sell your idea.

When I shared this secret with my friend and colleague Mark Victor Hansen – co-creator of the *Chicken Soup for the Soul©* series – he started sharing it with all his seminar participants. In fact, I'd like to share with you what Mark said happened in his seminar …

****

Mark's Story

We had a lady at our seminar that I asked this question I learned from Phil. And, she was pregnant. And, she said, "Mr. Gates, we're in the elevator here together. You can see I'm pregnant. Just put your hand on my belly. I just want to tell you that I was adopted. And, what I want do is be the spokesperson to adopt every kid in the world, so we make sure that every kid's loved. Now, as you can feel the baby kicking, you could get behind that couldn't you."

See, it's that quick – if it's your soul-force energy. Don't you all have goosebumps! 'Cause … remember I'm in the business of selling positive goosebumps. Is there anyone here who if you were Bill Gates wouldn't go for that?

43

She just did it spontaneously. What Phil and I are saying - if you're authentic, if you're living at your soul-force energy, you're irresistible.

****

Thank you, Mark.

I want you to be ready for the unique opportunities that will be coming your way. So take a few minutes right now and write a 50-word sales pitch script. Write down what you would say if you had 15 seconds with Bill Gates or Oprah Winfrey on the elevator. Make sure you add how much you need.

Your 50-Word Elevator Pitch

_____

_____

_____

_____

_____

_____

_____

Once you've written that down, I invite you to…

1. Give your sales pitch to the next 2 people you meet. Make sure that you stick to just 15 seconds.

2. When you finish, ask them what grabbed their attention.

3. Write down what they say.

Before we end today's Secret, I want to share another story with you. This really happened to a colleague of mine. She actually got on the elevator with Bill Gates. It happened a while ago at the time when Microsoft was engaged in some hefty lawsuits. My colleague is quite intuitive. She sensed some tension in the air.

Instead of focusing on herself and her 15-second elevator pitch, she said, "I'm sorry to hear about all the legal difficulties you're having. It must be a stressful time." This must have been the perfect thing to say, because she was then invited to spend the rest of the afternoon with Mr. Gates and his associates.

So, have your 15-second elevator spiel ready!

In review, you never know when you'll run into a potential donor or someone who might connect you with a potential donor. Take a few minutes right now to write down what you would say if you got on an elevator with a Warren Buffet, Bill Gates or Oprah Winfrey. Then, share your 15-second elevator pitch with the next 2 people you meet. Then, listen to what grabbed their attention.

This concludes Secret 11. In the next secret, you'll learn why it's important to assess the needs of your community before you begin writing your grant proposal.

Secret 12 – Assess The Needs Of Your Community First

A winning grant proposal must include an understanding of your organization's own needs and strengths, as well as your community's needs and strengths. This Secret includes 5 reasons why it is important for you to assess the needs of your community first. It also includes 5 key elements of a good needs assessment and an example of a community needs assessment that resulted in getting a grant.

Why is it important to assess the needs of your community first?

5 Reasons to Access the Community's Needs First

Here are 5 reasons to assess the community's needs first:

Reason 1 – You will avoid duplication of other projects doing similar things elsewhere.

Reason 2 – You can determine the "most pressing" of all the problems and needs first. By prioritizing the most pressing needs first, you have a greater chance of success, and success more quickly. Instead of spreading yourself out too thin, you focus on what's at the top of your list first. With a success or two under your belt, you can attract more funding to address the other "less pressing" problems later.

Reason 3 – You are in a better position to leverage and maximize the resources you have within your agency and community.

Reason 4 – You are able to determine the 'impact' of getting a grant. Most people don't realize the negative "side effects" of getting a grant or contract. These are often unexpected. For example, you may experience a change in the structure of your organization, personnel may have to be terminated later (unless sustained funding is secured), priorities may have to be changed, and there is likely to be an impact on the facilities and equipment.

Reason 5 – You can better be able to justify the need for your project and grant if you assess the community's needs first.

A "needs assessment" is a survey instrument that's used prior to seeking funding. It's a tool you can use to determine the needs and interests for your agency, your agency's clients, as well as the community overall.

5 Key Elements Of A Good "Needs Assessment"

A good needs assessment should have these 5 components:

1. A clear, concise statement of the problem in your community that your grant will try to solve.

2. An accurate description of the population to be served by your grant.

3. A list of factors or specific reasons why your idea should be prioritized over other requests for funding. In other words, why should your project to be funded and others not.

4. A summary of the literature, the research and any other studies that have addressed this same problem, as well as a summary of other programs which have tried to address this same problem in a different context elsewhere.

5. Mention any additional data that you propose to collect during your project.

Example: All-In-One Community Center

Let's look at an example …

A colleague of mine worked for a city government in a neighboring state. They conducted a confidential survey of the citizens and asked for their priorities in making the city a better place to live.

The response was nearly unanimous from all the citizens. Not only did the community want a community center, but over 70% requested senior services, as well as a youth center with structured activities for the city's youth.

With the results of the needs assessment, the city created a Community Action Plan Task Force. They met monthly and it was comprised of local business leaders, senior citizens and youth, it included the City Council, and other concerned citizens.

The Task Force recommended creating a facility that would house the Community Center. Collectively, the community members recommended moving a donated historical train depot from its present location to a new site where construction of the New City Hall and an all-in-one Community Center could take place.

With a strong needs assessment and community action plan, the city was approached by the Ford Foundation who agreed to fund the project. So, if you are serious about addressing the needs in your community, conduct a needs assessment, first.

In review, a well-developed grant proposal should include an understanding of your organizations own needs and strengths, as well as your community's needs and strengths. A common instrument that's used to assess the needs is called a "needs assessment." Do it prior to seeking funding, and you'll increase your chances that your proposal would be funded.

This concludes Secret 12. In the next secret, we'll take a look at what a fundable plan looks like. In other words, we'll take a look at what the key sections of a fundable plan should be.

Checklist: Needs Assessment

☐ A clear, concise statement of the problem in your community that your grant will try to solve.

_____

_____

☐ An accurate description of the population to be served by your grant.

_____

_____

☐ A list of factors or specific reasons why your idea should be prioritized over other requests for funding.

Factor:_____   Factor:_____

Reason:_____   Reason:_____

☐ A summary of literature, research and studies that have addressed this same problem, as well as a summary of other programs which have tried to address this same problem in a different context elsewhere.

_____

_____

☐ Mention any additional data that you propose to collect during your project.

_____

_____

Secret 13 – The 8 Basic Sections Of A Winning Proposal

So, let's get started.

There are eight basic sections of the world's most commonly used winning format:

1. Summary;

2. Introduction of Agency;

3. Problem Statement;

4. Project Objectives;

5. Project Methods;

6. Project Evaluation;

7. Future Funding or Sustainability; and

8. Budget.

My intention for including these eight sections right now is so that you get an overview of the key sections. For practice, I do recommend two different templates: one for corporate and foundation grants that are 1-4 pages and another template for government grants. But, I'll give you more information about that later.

Let's look at the key sections of a proposal. And, this includes any proposal.

Section 1 - The Summary

Your proposal summary outlines your project and should appear at the beginning of your proposal. It could be in the form of a cover letter or a separate page, but it should be brief - no longer than two or three paragraphs.

It's most useful if you write it after you've written the rest of the proposal because it encompasses all the key summary points necessary to communicate the basic idea of your project. It is this section that becomes the cornerstone of your proposal. And, the initial impression that it gives will be critical to your success. In many cases, the summary will be the first part of the proposal seen by agency officials and very possibly could be the only part of the package that is carefully reviewed before the decision is made to consider the project any further.

As mentioned in previous Secrets, you must select a fundable project which can be supported in view of the local needs in your community.

Let's look at Section 2.

Section 2 – The Introduction to Your Agency

You want to present yourself as a credible applicant. You should gather data about your organization from all available sources. Most proposals require a description of an applicant's organization to describe its past and present operations. Here are 3 features to consider:

1. A brief biography of board members and key staff members.

2. The organization's goals, philosophy, track record and other grantors, and even success stories.

3. The data should be relevant to the goals of the Federal grant agency or the Foundation or Corporate agency and should establish your credibility.

Section 3 - The Problem Statement

The problem statement - or what's sometimes referred to as the "needs assessment" - is a key element of your proposal. It makes a clear, concise, and well-supported statement of the problem that you're addressing.

The best way to collect information about the problem is to conduct a formal or informal needs assessment in your service area. The information provided should be both factual and directly related to the problem addressed by your proposal.

If you're looking for ways to conduct a needs assessment, any local, regional or state government planning office or local university offering course work in planning and evaluation techniques should be able to provide excellent background references. The types of data that you might collect include: historical, geographic, quantitative, factual, statistical, and philosophical information, as well as studies completed by colleges, and literature searches from public and university libraries.

Local colleges and universities which have a department or section related to your specific topic may be helpful in determining if there is interest in developing a student or faculty project to help you with conducting a needs assessment.

Section 4 - Project Objectives or Your Desired Outcomes

Program objectives refer to the specific activities in your proposal. It is necessary to identify all the objectives related to the goals to be reached, and what kinds of methods that you want to use to reach your goals. Consider quantities or things that are measurable and refer to the problem statement and the outcome of your proposal activities when developing a well-stated objective.

Remember, if the proposal is funded, the stated objectives will probably be used to evaluate the program's progress, so be realistic. If writing clear, concise measurable objective is something that you don't have experience in, then I invite you to take one of our classes.

Section 5 – Project Methods

This is your "action plan." These are the activities and the activity timeline that we talked about in the previous Secrets. The activities that occur along with the related resources and staff needed should be included in this section.

You might want to include a flow chart of the organizational features of your project.

Whenever possible, you want to justify in the narrative why you chose a specific method or specific activity. A PERT chart might be useful in supporting and justifying your proposal. PERT stands for Program Evaluation and Review Technique.

Also, you want to highlight the innovative features of your proposal.

Section 6 - Evaluation

The evaluation of your proposal is really done in two main ways:

1. You evaluate the 'product'; and

2. You evaluate the 'process'.

Product evaluation addresses the results that can be 'attributed' to the project that you did, as well as the extent to which your project actually satisfied its desired outcomes. The process evaluation addresses 'how' the project was conducted. It addresses the consistency of your stated action plan and your activity timeline and the effectiveness of the various activities within your plan.

Section 7 - Future Funding

This is your Sustainability Plan. Refer to Secret 10 for 21 strategies for a Killer Sustainability Plan. Describe your plan for continuing beyond the grant period. What's the availability of other resources that are necessary to implement your grant? Discuss any maintenance or future program funding that's necessary if it's for construction or purchase of equipment.

Section 8 - Budget

A well-prepared budget justifies all expenses and is aligned and consistent with your proposal narrative. In the budget section, you want to break down the costs that you're requesting, as well as any costs or expenses that are donated from other sources. When it's donated from another source, it's often times called 'matching' or 'in-kind'.

Here are 2 important things to consider when you're looking at your budget:

1. Does it include a brief, budget narrative that describes each expense? In other words, do you have 1-2 sentences that describe each expense?

2. Is it detailed? If you're requesting in your budget – 'office space' or 'rent' – it's helpful to include the cost per square foot. Also, if you include 'travel' in your budget, what's the local mileage rate for the project director. In other words, what's the cost per mile? And, how many miles is needed to travel per month?

In review, there are 8 basic sections of a winning proposal:

1. Summary;

2. Introduction To Your Agency;

3. Problem Statement;

4. Project Objectives;

5. Project Methods;

6. Project Evaluation;

7. Future Funding (Or Sustainability Plan); and

8. Budget.

This concludes Secret 13. It also concludes our first of the four steps of the grant proposal writing process. Remember: the first step is to Develop Your Idea. In the last 9 Secrets, we focused on how to develop your idea into a fundable proposal.

The next step is to Research Funders. Once we've developed our idea into a fundable proposal – which is step 1 of the grant proposal writing process – we're ready to start looking for funders. That's Step 2 – Researching Funders. So, the next nine secrets have to do with Researching Funders.

Next time, we're going to look at the best ways to identify potential funders whose ideas match yours.

Checklist: Proposal Evaluation Form

1 - Summary *Summarizes request clearly and concisely*	Yes	No	Score
1. Includes agency credibility			
2. Includes problem			
3. Includes measurable outcome			
4. Includes solution or method			
5. Includes cost			
2 - Agency Introduction - *Describes applicant's qualifications & credibility*	Yes	No	
1. Describes applying agency's mission and goals			*10 points*
2. Describes applying agency's clients, programs and activities			
3. Provides applying agency's accomplishments and qualifications			
3 - Problem or Needs Statement – *Shows need or problem to be solved*	Yes	No	
1. Includes statistical support – national & local			*25 points*
2. Is original			
3. Is timely			
4. Is compelling			
5. Makes "no" unsupported assumptions			
4 - Measurable Outcomes – *Establishes benefits in measurable terms*	Yes	No	
1. Describes the client/population that will benefit			*15 points*
2. Is written in measurable terms			
3. Includes by when and how outcome will be measured			
5 - Solution or Method – *Describes activities that will constitute a solution*	Yes	No	
1. Includes list of activities that constitute the solution			*10 points*
2. Includes reasons for selecting these activities			
3. Includes activity timeline			
4. Provides list of staff and brief staff job descriptions			

6 - Evaluation – *Provides plan to measure outcomes & method followed*	Yes	No	
1. *Process* evaluation – Shows how activities/timeline will be evaluated			10 *points*
2. *Product* evaluation – Shows how outcomes will be measured/reported			
7 - Future funding – *Describes sustainability plan beyond grant period*	Yes	No	
1. Includes a Sustainability Plan			10 *points*
2. Includes letters of support or commitments			
8 - Budget – *Provides detailed breakdown of costs requested & donated*	Yes	No	
1. Includes a budget narrative – describes each expense			20 *points*
2. Is detailed			
3. Includes requested, donated and total columns			
4. Is free of potential red flag expenses			
5. Includes indirect costs, if applicable			

_____   _____Total Points _____

Signature   Date   100 *points*

STEP 2
RESEARCH FUNDERS

Secret 14 – Lower Your Risk Of Failure In Getting A Grant

In this Secret and the next 8, we'll focus on the 2nd step of the grant proposal writing process; that is, Researching Funders. In Secret 14, we'll specifically lower your risk of failure.

To get a success rate greater than 93%, I follow the system outlined in this secret. You lower your risk of failure in getting funding by identifying funding prospects who are the best "matches" for you.

The best funding prospects for you are those who match you in at least 4 of these 5 categories: Interest, Support, Agency, Geography and Special population. I call this ISAGS: Interest, Support, Agency, Geography and Special population. This Secret includes the top 3 ways to locate the best funding match and 5 action steps you can take right now to lower your risk of failure.

5 Match Categories

The 5 funding matches are, as I said, I.S.A.G.S. = Interest, Support, Agency, Geography and Special population.

- So, Interest means by idea, subject, field or area of interest. That's the first category. (I)

- The second category – Support - means by type of support. What kinds of support do you need? Or, what kind of support are they (funders) willing to pay for? (S)

- Agency – 'A' – is by type of Agency. What type of agency do you have? And, what type of agency is the funder interested in giving money to? (A)

- 'G' is Geographic focus. What's the geographic focus of the funder? (G)

- The last one is 'S' as in Special population. What is the special population group that you're addressing? (S)

The presence of a 'match' in these categories will give you the quickest and the most accurate indication of your risk in applying. In other words, when there is a strong 'match', take it as a sign your risk of failure is lower. Go ahead and consider applying.

If "no match" exists, stop there. Your risk of failure is "too high."

Funders tell us that as much as 80% of the proposals they receive don't match their funding priorities. Don't be in this 80% group. Don't waste your time or the funder's. When "no match" exists, cut your losses and move on. Look instead for another funder whose is a "good match" for you.

You'll learn about these 5 Match Categories in Secret 15.

3 Top Ways To Find A Match

Here are 3 top ways to find a good match:

1. Use the Best Keywords - There are some excellent electronic databases and printed resources that show you exactly how funder's think and spend their money. These databases and resources use categories like the 5 that I just mentioned, as well as keywords within each category based on funding choices and history. So, identify up front all the keywords in the 5 Match Categories.

2. Understand the 4 Funder Types – By understanding the 4 types of funders – foundations, corporations, government agencies and individual donors – you will be able to discern very quickly the best funder who is best suited for you.

3. Use Linear and Non-Linear Approaches - It is helpful to understand the linear and non-linear approaches to finding potential funders. With this information, the next steps you need to take to find potential funders whose ideas match yours should become very clear to you.

You'll learn how to use the best key words, understand the 4 funder types, and how to use linear and non-linear approaches in the next Secrets; that is, Secrets 15, 16, 17, 18, 19 and 20.

5 Action Steps To Lower Your Risk Of Failure

Step 1 – Research the Funding History – One way to do this is by checking the 990-PF – that's the tax return for non-profits. Find these for the funders you are considering.

Step 2 – Gather Application Forms and Guidelines - Once you've found some prospective funder – with a potentially good match – gather the application forms and guidelines. Government agencies often call their guidelines "requests for proposals" – or RFP's. Sometimes they also refer to them as "requests for applications" – or RFA's.

Step 3 – Conduct a Pre-Proposal Contact – Conduct a pre-proposal contact with a funding official to get as much information as you can that will help you customize your proposal.

Step 4 - Contact a Previous Grantee – You'll probably identify these in your pre-proposal contact of Step 3.

Step 5 – Decide "Yes" or "No" – Pull together all the information you collected in steps 1-4. Ultimately, narrow down your search to a 'yes' or 'no' answer. Is this funder a "good match" for you? 'Yes' or 'No'?

In review, there are 5 Match Categories. We use the acronym ISAGS, which stands for Interest, Support, Agency, Geography and Special population. There are 3 top ways to find a match: first, find the perfect keywords; second, understand the 4 funder types; and third, use the linear and non-linear approaches.

There are also 5 action steps that will lower your risk of failure …

1. Research Funding History.

2. Gather Application Forms and Guidelines.

3. Conduct a Pre-Proposal Contact.

4. Contact a Previous Grantee.

5. Decide 'Yes' or 'No'.

We will begin to focus on all of these areas in the next secrets. In the next secret, we'll focus on the 5 matches and how to find the perfect keywords for your funding search.

Secret 15 – Find The Perfect Keywords For Your Search

In Secret 14, we discussed that the best funding prospects for you are those who match you in at least the first 4 of these 5 categories: Interest, Support, Agency, Geography and Special populations. I use the acronym ISAGS.

Let's delve further into these 5 ISAGS categories. We'll also look at one example of how you could use keywords to research your idea, as well as where to find a "hard copy" of the publications and electronic databases that will speed up your funder research.

At the beginning of your research for potential funders, it is very useful to identify the most important keywords or the key data fields that relate to your idea. *Keywords* are "words and phrases commonly used to categorize grants and funding" ...

- First, by the idea, subject, field and area of Interest - we call that the 'I' = Interest;
- Also, by type of Support you need. The 'S' for Support.
- By type of Agency as in 'A'.
- By Geographic focus = 'G', and
- By Special population, the 'S'.

Getting good at matching in these five categories will narrow your research quickly and guide you to potential funders with maximum ease.

Many publications and electronic databases use such words and fields to categorize grants and funder information. Identifying keywords up front will save you time by helping you scan through the piles of data quickly and go directly to the information you need.

So, let's look at an example. Flip to your Keyword List (at the end of this Secret 15). Now, all the keywords were listed in Secret 2. If you would like digital, 8 ½ x 11 versions of all checklists and worksheets in this book, as well as some new ones, visit **PhilJohncock.com/4-Steps**.

So, with a Keyword List checklist in hand, we're going to go through these, and I'll give you an example for my idea of providing "job training."

In the Subject/Field of Interest category, you're asked to circle your subject or field of interest. So, for my "job training" project, I'm going to circle 'education', 'employment'- and there's another category that doesn't exist here but it might show up occasionally in our research called 'training' - so, education, employment and training.

The next category is Types of Support. It says, "Circle the type of support you are looking for." In this case, it's helpful to know exactly what you need. Have on hand a list of items in your budget and what you need for your project. So, I'm going to give you a few from mine. I've circled "conferences or seminars," "consulting services," "curriculum development" - these are all things that I need to fund for my project - "employee-related scholarships," "general/operating support," "internship funds," "seed money," and "sponsorships."

So, these are the types of support that I'm looking for for this particular project.

Now, the third category is Type of Recipient. And, the instructions say, "Circle your recipient type." Now, I've circled for my "job training" idea the recipient of "educational institutions," as well as "professional societies and associations."

The Geographic focus … The instructions say, "List your geographic focus" or where your project is going to be. This refers to the primary interest of the funder: the city, county, region, state, national or international. So, I'm going to put down in my city (blank): "<u>Reno</u>" or "<u>Sparks</u>". The county is "<u>Washoe</u>". And, the state is "<u>Nevada</u>". And, the region is "<u>West</u>" or "<u>Western States</u>."

In the Special Populations category, the instructions say, "Circle any special populations you plan to serve." So, I'm going to circle "men and boys" primarily, "minorities". There's another category that may be a special population that I'm going to use is "unemployed".

The bottom portion of this Keyword List refers to Funder Prospect Brainstorming. And, the instructions say, "List possible matches as you progress in your future research." So, in the upcoming Secrets, we're going to talk about corporations, foundations, government agencies and individual donors. As we progress through the next 4 Secrets, you can list possible matches as you begin to 'brainstorm' those particular funders.

Making your idea fit as many of these categories as possible - without losing the overall integrity of your idea - will bring you many more funders with potential idea matches.

Now that we have identified our keywords, let's take the next step. We're going to look at the hard-copy publications and electronic databases for our funder research.

Funder Hard-Copy Publications And Electronic Databases

A common question that I'm asked is, "What are the best hard-copy publications and electronic databases to use for your funder research?" Before I give you a direct answer, let me provide you (with) a couple of insights.

One of the biggest problems with any publication is once it is published, it is already outdated. New funder information comes along to make the published data obsolete. A common mistake for new grant writers is that they take the published information at face value and stop there. They assume that it's the most accurate, most up-to-date information.

Let me give you an example. I have a book of funders for small businesses and entrepreneurs right now on my desk. It's written by "the nation's leading authority," according to the book. The book was originally published in 1988, then again three more times, with the last publication in 1995.

Having been in the publishing business for 7 years now, I know that it takes months, even years sometimes for a large publisher to get the finished manuscript printed and then distributed. So, if you were to get this book hot off the presses, the information between its covers is already several years outdated.

O.K. Let's say that you take the information in the book at face value, and you send a letter of inquiry to the address in the book. This address is for a funder in Nevada, where I live now. You include the contact person listed for that funder in the book because you didn't check further. It just so happens that the contact person is no longer working for the foundation, and the new person isn't happy because the letter comes addressed to the former person. One strike against you.

Let's say that you use an electronic database of funders. Your eyes light up because you see tons of potential donors. But, where did this data come from?

After some digging, you find out that it's a 10-year old database of 990-PF tax returns that keeps old returns on file and hasn't updated them in years. In other words, the database you're looking at doesn't have the most accurate, up-to-date information. So, you don't get the most recent funding priorities, and you submit an application - only to find out that the funder stopped funding that special population or geographic area six years ago.

Out-dated and inaccurate information are just two possible problems that happen with hard-copy publications and electronic databases. Getting current and accurate funder information is a challenge to all funder researchers. And, we haven't even talked about getting funding information on the Internet using search engines like Google, Yahoo and MSN. The Internet has made it easier to get "certain information" faster. But, it means that the information has to be accurate and updated by people. But, grant funding information is woefully slow.

So, now here's my answer to the original question:

For new grant writers, I suggest that you stick with the "tried-and-true" resources from the Foundation Center at FoundationCenter.org. It's been around longer than most. Plus, the Foundation Center has Free Funding Information Centers spread out all over the U.S. in libraries, community foundations and foundations. They have one or more in each state. These are called "Cooperating Collections." There you can go and research the online database as well as the hard-copy publication that are the most accurate and up-to-date you'll find on the market. And, it's FREE. Don't pay for anything until you're sure you'll get your money's worth.

When I published my first book on grant proposal writing in 2003, I included a list of all the Cooperating Collections at the time. That list has changed and more Cooperating Collections have been added, and some have been dropped. I know this because I spoke last Friday with the Coordinator of the Cooperating Collections.

To give you an example, in 2003, there were two Cooperating Collections in Nevada, one in the north and one in the south. Today, there is one still in the south, but three new ones in the north.

What's important to remember is that there are FREE funding information "hard copy" publications and online databases at your fingertips that you can access directly from your local Cooperating Collection - all for FREE.

I recommend that you start there. Go to FoundationCenter.org and search for Cooperating Collections. At the time of recording this Secret, there's a map of all 50 states and the names, addresses and phone numbers of the latest Cooperating Collections, as well as a downloadable .PDF.

Action Steps

So, I want you to locate the Cooperating Collection closest to you. Set up an appointment to visit, and use their online funder database. I want you to use your keywords as a starting point.

So, in review, to find the perfect keywords for you and begin your funder research, take these 4 steps:

1. Step 1 - Print out your Keyword List.

2. Step 2 - Circle the keywords for your idea.

3. Step 3 - Locate the Cooperating Collection nearest you by going to FoundationCenter.org and searching for "Cooperating Collections."

4. Step 4 - Set up an appointment to visit your Cooperating Collection. Use their online database.

This concludes Secret 15. In the next secret, we'll focus on corporate funders and how to approach corporate funders strategically.

Checklist – Keywords for Funder Research

Idea_____Date_____

CIRCLE   ALL THAT APPLY

SUBJECT/FIELD OF INTEREST – *Circle your subject or field of interest*

Agriculture/food, animals/wildlife, arts/humanities, civic rights, community development, crime/law enforcement, education, employment, environment, health care, health organizations, housing/shelter, human services, international affairs, international giving, medical research, mental health/crisis services, mutual aid societies, philanthropy/voluntarism, population groups, public affairs, recreation, religion, safety/ disasters, science, social sciences and youth development.

TYPES OF SUPPORT – *Circle the type of support you are looking for*

Annual campaigns, building/renovation, capital campaigns, cause-related marketing, conferences/ seminars, consulting services, continuing support, curriculum development, debt reduction, donated equipment, donated land, donated products, emergency funds, employee matching gifts, employee volunteer services, employee-related scholarships, endowments, equipment, exchange programs, fellowships, general/operating support, grants to individuals, in-kind gifts, internship funds (institutional support), land acquisition, loaned talent, matching/ challenge support, professorships, program development, program evaluation, program-related investments/loans, public relations services, publication, research, scholarship funds (institutional support), scholarships (to individuals), seed money, sponsorships, student loans (to individuals), technical assistance, and use of facilities.

TYPE OF RECIPIENT – *Circle your recipient type*

Animal-specific agencies, arts/humanities organizations, churches/temples, civil rights groups, community improvement organizations, disease-specific health associations, educational institutions, environmental agencies, federated funds, government agencies, hospitals/medical care facilities, human service agencies, international organizations, media organizations, medical research institutes, mental health agencies, museums/historical societies, performing arts groups, professional societies and associations, public administration agencies, public general health organizations, public policy institutes, recreation organizations, research institutes, science organizations, social science organizations, technical assistance centers, and youth development agencies.

GEOGRAPHIC FOCUS – *List your geographic focus*

Usually relates to location of primary interest of the funder: city, county, region, state, national/international

City_____   County_____

State_____   Region_____

SPECIAL POPULATIONS – *Circle any special populations you plan to serve*

Aging, alcohol and drug abusers, children and youth, crime or abuse victims, disabled, economically disadvantaged, homeless, immigrants and refugees, men and boys, military and veterans, minorities, offenders and ex-offenders, people with AIDS, single parents, women and girls

FUNDER PROSPECT BRAINSTORMING – *List possible matches as you progress in your future research*

Corporations   _____ _____

Foundations   _____ _____

Government agencies _____ _____

Individual donors   _____ _____

Secret 16 – Approach Corporations Strategically

While exact numbers are not reported annually, according to *Giving USA*, in 2008 U.S. corporations gave $14.5 billion in tax-exempt contributions to nonprofits. In this Secret, you'll discover important corporate giving facts - including the Law of Surplus - that will assist you in your grant proposal writing.

Corporate Giving Facts

Here are 7 corporate giving facts …

Fact 1 - In 1999, of the more than 5 million corporations in the U.S. at the time, only 35% made philanthropic contributions.

Fact 2 - Of those that did make contributions, only a small percent contributed more than $500 annually.

Fact 3 - As privately-owned businesses, corporations have no obligation to disseminate information about their philanthropic activities. They are responsible to stockholders not the general public. Finding where grant information from corporations is may be challenging.

Fact 4 - Corporations give where they live. In other words, they usually have a geographic focus where their plants are located. The plants, workers, products and other vested interests play a significant role in corporate giving.

Ask a worker to check for you to see what grant funding is available. That may be the easiest approach to use. It's easier for a worker to ask for information than an outsider.

Fact 5 - Since company donations depend on the company's profitability and its charitable and marketing budgets, your funder research should include both charitable and marketing budgets.

Fact 6 - Some have created their own Corporate Foundations, like Wal-Mart and AT&T. They are particularly responsive to the needs of their workers and communities where they live and have plant operations, as said previously. Specify what you have to offer that will affect their workers, products, corporate concerns, and geographic focus.

Fact 7 – It's often easier for corporations – and individuals, too - to give non-monetary goods than it is money, especially with tightening budgets. This is called the Law of Surplus. A common mistake many beginning grant writers make is to focus solely on asking for money and don't take advantage of the Law of Surplus. I made this mistake for at least 8 years.

The Law Of Surplus

The Law of Surplus states that corporations are more likely to give what they have a 'surplus' of. If they have a surplus of profits, they are able to give money. If they have employees, they might be able to donate labor for a fundraiser or special event. You may have seen this when a corporation adopts an agency. If they have a surplus of products and services, they are prime candidates for you to approach for tangible items you need for your projects.

The Law of Surplus also states that if there is no longer a surplus in one place, don't waste your time looking there. Instead, look for where the surplus is. In other words, if the surplus of profits is gone and corporations, like individuals, are tightening their finance belts, it is less likely for them to give money. Why? Because there is 'no' surplus to draw from.

However, it doesn't take much effort to find the gold mind of surpluses of goods hidden from your view. For example, a restaurant might be willing to prepare and donate food for a fundraising event. A conference center or college might donation a room while musicians donate music and entertainment. Likewise, a construction company may be willing to donate building supplies, even labor, to help renovate classrooms.

Here's an example …

One student told me that she was having "no luck" getting a grant for $85,000 she needed for fencing. You see, she had an animal shelter, and the wolves were digging beneath the wooden fences they had. What they needed was a metal fence buried far enough that the wolves couldn't dig under.

Instead of asking for money - like she was doing unsuccessfully - I invited her instead to look for a surplus of what she actually needed, which was 'fencing'. Who has a surplus of 'fencing'? Well, the answer is "a fencing manufacturer."

The Law of Surplus says that if a surplus of money isn't readily available, try a surplus in another area. She found a business who not only donated the fencing, but the labor to install it. She didn't need money after all. She needed fencing. And, she got it! $85,000 worth of fencing and labor - everything donated!

The point is that corporations are great sources of surpluses for what you need. You can take advantage of the Law of Surplus by focusing first on what you need. Then, ask, "Who has a surplus of this?" Keep in mind that there is very likely a corporation someplace who has a surplus of what you need - the very product you need - right now.

By sharing their surplus with you, they are donating something they actually have. Their out-of-pocket expenses are limited while the benefits of giving are not.

In summary, one way to strategically use corporations is to maximize the power of the Law of Surplus to your advantage. Look first for non-money donations.

2 Challenges: 1 Work And 1 Personal

Now, here are 2 challenges for you: one that's a work challenge, and one that's a personal challenge. Here's your work challenge. Let's call it the "80% challenge": challenge yourself and your agency to *get at least 80% of the items you need for your next project donated*. Then, leverage the donations to ask for actual money.

In other words, once you get things donated, when you ask for money, you can show that 80% has already been donated by other corporations. This makes it super easy for a funder to say, 'yes' to the remaining 20% that you need (money) because you've gotten the rest donated. How can they refuse when there is so much already donated!

Here's your personal challenge: *identify the surpluses you have* personally, like clothes, movies, maybe some extra time, like four hours a month. Then, find creative ways to use the Law of Surplus to give away your surplus to a needy charity. You can give your clothes to the Salvation Army, your surplus of movies to the local library, your extra four hours a month to the local soup kitchen for the homeless. Today, I just donated some organic sodas to a local church.

6 Corporate Research Strategies

Here are 6 corporate research strategies - that is, 6 strategies you can use when you're looking for corporate funding:

Strategy 1 - Know what information to look for (i.e., officers, trustees, headquarters, and the operation locations).

Strategy 2 - Use the Internet – Try using the FoundationCenter.org, the Thomas Register, and the company's own website.

Strategy 3 - Use business directories.

Strategy 4 - Check the Foundation Center and the Cooperating Collections - If the corporation has an established foundation, then a good resource is the Foundation Center at FoundationCenter.org and also the closest Cooperating Collection. Foundation Center "hard-copy" publications of interest might be the *National Directory of Corporate Giving* and *Corporate Foundation Profiles.* These publications, as well as IRS tax returns and other resources, can be found in your local Cooperating Collection.

Strategy 5 - To research accurate information about the company's profitability, use Dun and Bradstreet – Find someone who subscribes to Dun and Bradstreet's financial services. Ask them to request a Dun and Bradstreet report on the prospective corporate funder. The report you get will tell you the fiscal stability of the company.

Strategy 6 - Also, buy one share of stock - Another technique for researching local corporations is to purchase one share of stock in each publicly held company in your area. Watch your dividend checks. If you get one, you will know the company is making a profit. You will also get the latest information on the corporate administrators and board member changes.

In review, there are 7 facts to keep in mind as you develop your corporate giving plan, such as understanding the Law of Surplus and using it to your advantage. Also, this Secret includes 7 corporate research strategies, including buying one share of stock to get accurate information about a company's profitability.

This concludes Secret 16.

In the next secret, we'll explore what foundations are and how to approach them strategically.

Secret 17 – Approach Foundations Strategically

According to *Giving USA*, Foundations gave $41.21 Billion in grants in 2008. In this Secret, you'll discover important foundation giving facts that will assist you in your grant proposal writing and your research.

8 Foundation Giving Facts

Here are 8 foundation giving facts that will help you in your grant proposal writing and in your research …

Fact 1 – There are over 90,000 grant-making U.S. foundations today.

Fact 2 – 90% of U.S. Foundations do not have websites.

Fact 3 - Although the figures vary slightly from year to year, the 4,000 largest foundations have 90 percent of the assets and make 80 percent of the awards.

Fact 4 - By federal law, foundations must give away 5 percent of the market value assets or interest income each year, whichever is higher. This law means, for example, that the W.K. Kellogg Foundation with over $8.4 billion in market assets must award at least $420 million annually.

Fact 5 - Most foundations must follow the 5 percent rule or risk losing their tax-exempt status. It's the law.

Fact 6 - Foundations vary considerably in market assets, staff size, funding priorities, review protocols, geographic giving patterns, and preferred approach.

Fact 7 - The five primary types of foundations are national, community, corporate, family, or special purpose. For example, some 'national' foundations are the Ford Foundation, W.K. Kellogg Foundation, and the Rockefeller Foundation. An example of a 'special purpose' foundation is the Whitaker foundation that restricts support to biomedical research.

Fact 8 - Some private foundations are eager to share information about themselves; others take a very constrained approach to information dissemination. Again, remember Fact 2… that 90% of U.S. Foundations do not have websites.

6 Foundation Research Tips

Here are 6 foundation research tips that you can use …

Tip 1 - Network. Pay special attention to those people who mention board memberships or friends on foundation boards.

Tip 2 - Consider how your idea fits into the mostly commonly funded areas, like education, health, human services, public and society benefit, arts and culture, international affairs, religion, environment and animals.

Tip 3 - Contact staff. Less than 8% of all foundations have staff who are employed to manage their granting programs. Many required contact by letter.

Tip 4 - Use foundation directories, electronic retrieval systems, and database searches, as well as the foundation websites, themselves. However, when you look at the foundation websites, be careful because they may be months, even a year or two outdated. Most of your research can be done online or at your local Free Cooperating Collection. To find the Cooperating Collections nearest you, go to FoundationCenter.org and search for "Cooperating Collections."

Tip 5 - Use the foundation's 990-PF tax return. This IRS information is public; it contains assets, grants paid or committed for future payments, and managers.

Tip 6 - Collect 3 important pieces of information: 1) the net assets, 2) the list of key personnel like staff and officers, and 3) list of recipients of grants for the previous year.

In review, there are 7 foundation giving facts including that most foundations must follow the 5 percent rule or risk losing their tax-exempt status. It's the law. There are 6 foundation research tips, such as using the foundation 990-PF tax return, as well as gathering 3 important pieces of information: the net assets, the list of key personnel, as well as the list of recipients of grants for the previous year.

This concludes Secret 17.

So far, we've looked at the first two funder types: corporations and foundations. In the next secret, we'll focus on government grants and how to approach government agencies strategically.

Secret 18 – Approach Government Agencies Strategically

Although no single source of information covers all government grants, most federal agencies have some type of grant-making program. This Secret will help you become familiar with government grants by providing you with federal government grant facts and research tips, as well as the 8 main types of federal government grants.

4 Federal Government Grant Facts

So, here it is: four federal government grant facts ...

Fact 1 - In 2009, the American Recovery and Reinvestment Act – which is also called the Stimulus Package - injected a historic $463 Billion in additional grant funding into the grant pipeline.

Fact 2 - Federal government funding for grants varies from year to year. At the time of recording this Secret, it's around $100 Billion, depending on who you talk to. Despite a decline in the funding for social service, health, and welfare programs in the mid-to-late 1980s, over a 20-year period starting in 1980, the U.S. government funding for grants more than doubled. It increased from $40 Billion to $90 Billion.

Fact 3 - According to the Catalog of Federal Domestic Assistance, there are 1,999 federal assistance programs at the time of this recording.

Fact 4 - There are 64 federal granting departments and agencies at the time of this recording. The top 5 grant-making departments – in terms of the grant programs they offer – are the Department of Health and Human Services (376), the Department of Agriculture (229), the Department of The Interior (203), Department of Education (168), and the Department of Justice (124).

4 Government Research Tips

Here are the 4 government research tips to help you …

Tip 1 - Find the Organizational Chart - To find information about federal grant programs, familiarize yourself with the organizational structure of the government agencies. Check their website or ask for an organizational chart. Once you are familiar with the organizational structure, you can delve into appropriate reference materials that describe grant opportunities.

Tip 2 - Ask About Technical Assistance - Often, governmental agencies conduct training called *technical assistance* workshops. These are sessions to familiarize you with funding guidelines and priorities. They assist you with completing appropriate forms and applications. These are informative and provide grant writers with opportunities to meet the agency staff and ask questions.

Tip 3 - Contact Your U.S. Senator and Representative - Government officials are sometimes able to assist you in your grant proposal writing efforts. They can help search for funding for initiatives that they find particularly relevant to their constituents, their political platforms, and their geographic regions that they represent. They can even introduce new legislation to provide funding.

Tip 4 - Keep Taxpayers In Mind – Keep foremost in your mind that federal funds are the result of taxes paid by people like you and me. It's your responsibility to make sure you propose to spend these tax dollars as precisely and closely as you can and that everything is aligned with your project outcomes. Avoid padding budgets and rounding up numbers that might threaten your credibility.

8 Types of Federal Government Grants

Here are the 8 main types of federal government grants …

Type 1 - Block grants – Block grants are a large sum of money that is given from the federal government to a regional or state government with only general provisions on how the money has to be spent. Each region experiments with different ways to spend the money with the same goal in mind. Each region or state determines the process for distributing the funding. "Mental health services" block grants are examples of this type of funding.

Type 2 – Categorical grants – Categorical grants are more strict and have specified provisions from the federal government as to how money can be spent. In other words, there are more strings attached. Often, these funds are given directly to a state agency who distributes it state-wide. Examples of this include urban forestry assistance, hazardous abatement and other specific projects.

Type 3 – Competitive grants – Competitive grants are generally given directly by federal agencies. Therefore, it is likely you will apply directly to the federal agency, such as the National Endowment for the Arts. Most of these grants are used for specific purposes, such as scientific research, educational goals, social services, technological development, health care and arts related projects.

Type 4 - Earmark grants – Earmark grants are very specialized. They are government grants that are not given out on a competitive basis. Since these grants involve political lobbyists, there is a lot of debate about the security of these grants.

Type 5 – Formula grants – Formula grants are non-competitive awards based on a predetermined formula, such as your state's population. Therefore, each state receives money based on it's percentage of the total population of all the states. Each state, then, distributes the money within its boundaries. Examples of formula grants are funding for families raising children and those who need an employment training program.

Type 6 - Pell grants – Pell grants are scholarships provided to undergraduate students based on income level. They are distributed through a college or university.

Type 7 - Pork Barrel funding – You may have heard of Pork Barrel funding before, and you seldom refer to it as a 'grant', but it is 'grant-like'. It is government projects or appropriations set aside to generate jobs or provide some sort of benefit to a specific locale.

Type 8 – Title grants – Title grants are formula grants given to states according to provisions of a particular piece of legislation, such as TITLE I of the Elementary and Secondary Education Act of 1965. With the purpose of "improving the academic achievement of the disadvantaged," *Title I* was reauthorized under the No Child Left Behind Act of 2009. It provides resources to local schools. Another example is *Title IV* that provides grants to states for aid and services to needy families and children.

In review, most federal agencies have some type of grant-making program. Included in this Secret are 4 research tips, such as asking about technical assistance workshops that the agencies themselves provide. We ended with a description of the 8 main types of federal government grants: block grants, categorical grants, competitive grants, earmarks, formula grants, Pell grants, pork barrel funding and title grants.

This concludes Secret 18. In the next secret, we'll discuss individual donors and how to approach them strategically.

Secret 19 – Approach Individual Donors Strategically

Almost all the books on grant proposal writing ignore the topic of individuals as funders. Most resources for individual donations usually fall under the heading 'fundraising'.

The only reason I can see that individuals are left out of grant proposal writing discussions is because they seldom require formal written proposals. However, having a well-written letter or a well-written email, or even a newsletter can increase your individual donations.

Individual donations are a great form of "discretionary funds" which you cannot usually get with grants. In addition, if your goal is to diversify funding streams and sustain projects you start with grant seed money, then a discussion around individual donors and how they connect with foundations, corporations and government agencies is absolutely necessary.

4 Individual Donors Facts

Here are 4 individual donor facts …

Fact 1 - Individuals give more than the other 3 funder types combined. In other words, individuals give more than foundations, corporations and government agencies all together. According to *Giving USA*, individuals gave $206.62 Billion in donations in 2008.

Fact 2 - Individual 'bequests' are consistent source of funding, especially for churches and schools. *Giving USA* claims that individual bequests provided $22.66 Billion in 2008. Planned giving takes a lot of time to develop. But, it is one of the best sustainability strategies you can use.

Fact 3 - According to one expert fundraiser, around 89% of all individual donations come from people who make less than $150,000 a year.

Fact 4 - Donations from individuals are at the sole discretion of the donor. Discretionary funds are almost impossible to get from foundations, corporations and government agencies. Discretionary funds have "no strings attached." This means you can spend the money as you like.

3 Individual Donor Research Tips

Here are 3 individual donor research tips …

Tip 1 - Check out these 4 books:

1. *Where the Money Is: A Fund Raiser's Guide to the Rich* by Helen Bergan

2. *Who Knows Who: Networking Through Corporate Boards* by Jeanette Glynn

3. *Who's Who in America*

4. *Index to Who's Who Books*

These are 4 great books to check out regarding individual donors.

Tip 2 - If you've got the name of an individual who is associated with a particular foundation, check the *Guide to U.S. Foundations* or the online search at your local Cooperating Collections. There may be other online databases, as well, that provide extensive biographical information. Inquire at your local library or search online.

Tip 3 - For two proven approaches for fundraising and getting individual donations, I invite you to check out the books and programs by Terry Axelrod and Lynne Twist.

In review, individual donors give more than foundations, corporations and government agencies combined. Individual donations are a great source of discretionary funds. One place to look for long-term funding is individual bequests. Included in this Secret are 3 research tips for individual donors.

This concludes Secret 19.

Now that we've concluded our focus on the four funder types, we'll look at a linear (left-brained) and nonlinear (right-brained) approaches to finding funders.

Secret 20 – Use Linear & Nonlinear Approaches to Funders

In Secrets 16, 17, 18 and 19, we covered top facts and research tips about the four funder types: Corporations, Foundations, Government Agencies, and Individual Donors.

Today's Secret covers two unique ways to approach finding a potential funder from one of the four funder groups.

I call these approaches the left-brain and right-brain approaches. Each uses a different part of your brain. Both work well, and in fact, you should become familiar with both so you can take advantage of the qualities of both.

Let me explain …

Linear, Left-Brain Approach

The linear approach is the left-brained approach. The left-brain or linear approach is logical, sequential and rational. In this approach, you basically go out looking for the funders directly. You start by identifying potential funding sources that have a history of funding in your area. Once you identify one or more, you customize a proposal to the funder specifications.

Find out where funders distribute their guidelines and funding history. Identify potential funders and determine if your idea matches the funder's priorities. Draft a proposal with a budget. Ask for the full amount of what you need.

You might be asking "Where can you find funders 'directly'?"

The previous 4 Secrets provided some research tips that have proven successful over time. For example, since corporations have no obligation to make public their grant information, you may choose to contact a worker, or someone who knows a worker. Ask them to ask if the corporation has a grant.

For foundations, try using the online database available at your local Cooperating Collection. For government grants, contact the agency at the federal level that is most closely aligned with you and your interest. For example, if you work for a school, contact the Department of Education. For individual donors, check the *Guide to U.S. Foundations* or online search when you find an individual associated with a particular foundation.

These research tips are all linear and left-brained. What about the nonlinear or the right-brained approach?

Nonlinear, Right-Brained Approach

The right-brained or nonlinear approach is creative, intuitive and non-rational. Instead of you going out to find funders, funders literally find you. It is like the Law of Attraction, attracting funders to you.

How does it work?

Well, research shows that it starts with getting clear on what you want. We call it "developing your idea" first, and then making your idea more attractive to funders. The earlier Secrets like 4, 5, 6, 7, 8, and 9 provide tips for dreaming big and tapping into your passion. They also provide ways to make your ideas more timely, compelling and problem-solving.

The nonlinear approach also taps into the power of the concept of six degrees of separation.

6 Degrees of Separation

I'd like to share with you a story about **where the "six degrees of separation" comes from** …

It was the late 1960's, and a psychologist by the name of Stanley Milgram wanted to conduct an experiment to see how we human beings are connected. In his experiment, Milgram decided to send out a chain letter. He identified 160 people in Omaha, Nebraska. He sent them all a packet. In the packet was the name and home address of a stockbroker who worked in Boston, Massachusetts, and lived nearby.

Instructions in the packet told people to write their names on the packets and then send them to someone they knew who might get the packet to the stockbroker the fastest. So, if you had a relative in Boston, you might send the packet to him because you thought that he could get it to the stockbroker more quickly because he lived closer. You reason that your relative can get it to there in a fewer steps. Right?

Well, when all the packets arrived at the stockbroker's home, Milgram took the packets and counted how many names were on them. What he discovered was that **most of the packets had five or six names** on them. In essence, it usually took **five or six steps** to reach the stockbroker. This is where the six degrees of separation concept comes from.

Applying 6 Degrees of Separation to Funder Research (Step 2)

How does this apply to grant proposal writing and finding finders?

Well, the concept of six degrees of separation says that you are only six degrees - or six people - away from a potential funder. You never know when or where you might get a lead that will guide you to a funder or the funder to you. It's ideal to share your idea with as many people as possible.

The only exception that I know to this is to "not share with nay-sayers and devil's advocates." In other words, share with supportive and positive people, interested in your best interest.

Increase the number of eyes and ears who can bring you closer to a potential funder. Tell people you trust about your idea. Remember that others want you to be successful.

Identify a budget for what you want. Then, brainstorm creative ways to get what you want with existing resources, first, before you ask for money. In this way, you leverage your resources. Funders will take you more seriously.

Instead of looking for the money directly, focus on the idea and passion you have behind your dream. The questions to ask yourself is "What is your idea or dream?" and "Why are you passionate about it?" Build up your passion, the wind beneath your wings.

The nonlinear approach is based on universal, cyclical time. It is idea-based, not money-based.

In review, when thinking about the best way to approach finding funding for your idea, use both linear and nonlinear approaches. The linear or left-brain approach involves going directly to the sources for all four funders. The nonlinear or right-brain approach tells us to get clear about what we want, make our ideas more attractive to funders, share our ideas with others, and tap into the power of six degrees of separation.

This concludes Secret 20. In the next secret, we'll discuss how to double your chances of being funded by conducting a pre-proposal contact.

Secret 21 – Triple Your Chances Of Getting Your Grant Funding With A Pre-Proposal Contact

In a study of 10,000 federal proposals, the only variable that was statistically significant in separating the funded and rejected proposals was a pre-proposal contact with the funding source. This Secret focuses on the types of funders which do welcome an initial contact, as well as why it's important to make a pre-proposal contact and the 4 steps involved in the process.

Consider these 3 facts:

Fact 1 - According to the experts, your chances increase threefold when you contact the funding source before submitting your proposal.

Fact 2 - When it comes to government grants, officials usually welcome a pre-proposal contact. It saves them and you time.

Fact 3 - When it comes to private grants from corporations or foundations, sponsors vary in the receptivity to a pre-proposal contact. This is usually pointed out in their grant guidelines. In some cases, the preferred form of contact for private funders is a letter requesting grant information.

Why Make A Pre-Proposal Contact?

Pre-proposal contacts serve 3 primary purposes:

1. They verify the information you gathered during your search for a funder.

2. You can gather more information that will help you customize your proposal to the preferences of the funder.

3. You can make a positive first impression.

   Let's look at each of these in a little more detail …

1. Verify the information – Verifying the information you've gathered through your research is highly worthwhile. Since priorities change and deadlines shift, occasionally the information in reference books is inaccurate and outdated. Especially pay attention to the name of the contact person at the funding institution. This may have changed, as well.

2. Gather more information – Through a pre-proposal contact, you can get additional information. For example, knowing the funder's hidden agenda is key in writing a winning proposal. Also, find out who will review your application. Look for clues of what will appeal to the reviewer, as well as what you should avoid saying. You will need to gather the funder's applications and guidelines.

3. Make a positive first impression – Contacting the funder before you write your proposal allows you to make a very good first impression. If your organization is unknown to a funder, the pre-proposal contact is your first step in establishing credibility and letting the funder know who you are. The more you've done your homework, the more this will be reflected in the questions you ask – and the more impressed your contact person will be.

4 Steps of a Pre-Proposal Contact

There are 4 steps in the pre-proposal contact process that will give you the competitive edge. Here they are …

1. Ask for application forms and guidelines

2. Contact a past grantee

3. Contact a prior reviewer

4. Contact the funder representative

Let's look at each of these in more detail …

Step 1 – Ask for The Application Forms And Guidelines

If you can't get forms and guidelines online, ask for them. For government agencies you might be able to do it in person or over the phone. For private funders like foundations and corporations, you're probably going to need to write a letter.

In your letter, write "LETTER REQUESTING GRANT INFORMATION" at the top of the letter. This helps the person reading mail to be able to sort the nature of the letter quickly and get it into the right person's hands.

Enclose a self-addressed, stamped envelope. Avoid using "Dear Sir" or "To Whom It May Concern." That's a bad mistake. Instead, always address your cover letter to a specific person. Before you send it, make sure to verify the spelling of the names, titles and addresses.

Request a list of past grantees and reviewers. If you can't get the names of past reviewers, ask for their age, background and training, as well as how they were selected, their role in the review process, and the rating scale with points that were used in the evaluation process.

Step 2 - Contact a Past Grantee

Once you have a list of agencies who have received grants in the past, use it to analyze the previous grantees and the likelihood of your success. Some experts suggest that you look for four items:

1. Award Size – Identify the smallest and largest award, types of projects funded, and what does this tells you about the size of award you might receive.

2. Recipient Type – Look for the types of agencies that receive grants. Check how large and small they are, the common characteristics among last year's recipients, and any geographic preferences.

3. Project Director Degrees – Look at the academic degrees and titles that appear most often on the list of grantees. See if there is a correlation between the size of the award and the degrees held by the project director.

4. Choose 2 Past Grantees – Select two grantees to contact. If possible, choose organizations that you already know or have some sort of connection with.

Choose a past grantee outside your geographic area who is less likely to see you as a competitor. Explain how you got the grantee's name. Congratulate them on the award. Ask to speak with the grant writer who worked on the proposal.

Here is a list of 14 questions you might consider asking a past grantee …

1. Did you contact the funder prior to submitting your proposal?

2. Did you contact them by phone, letter or in person?

3. Who was the person most helpful on the funder's staff?

4. Did you use an outside consultant on the proposal?

5. Did you use an advocate or congress person?

6. Did you ask the funder to review an abstract of your proposal prior to its submission? If you did, what did they say?

7. Was there a hidden agenda in the applications or guidelines? If 'yes', what was it?

8. When did you start the application process?

9. When did you contact the funding source?

10. What resources did you find most useful in preparing your proposal?

11. Did the funder conduct a site visit of your program before or after the award? If so, find out who came, the age, what they wore, how old they were, the type of person – like were they conservative, moderate or liberal – and did anything surprise you in their visit?

12. How close was the approved budget to the one included in your original application?

13. Who negotiated the budget on the funder's staff?

14. What would you do differently next time?

Step 3 - Contact a Prior Reviewer

Many beginning and some expert grant writers shy away from asking for a list of prior reviewers or even contacting one. This one step can set your proposal apart from the rest.

Your goal is to learn as much as possible about the actual process used when reviewing proposals like yours. Here are 8 questions to ask a prior reviewer …

1. How did you become a reviewer?

2. Where did you review the proposal? At the funder's office or at your house?

3. Did you use an evaluation form and a point-based scoring system?

4. What were you asked to look for?

5. After being a reviewer, how would you write a proposal differently?

6. What were the most commonly-made mistakes?

7. Were you given a time limit? How much time did it take on an average to read the proposals?

8. Was there a staff review after the evaluation of proposals?

If you cannot get a list of grant reviewers, ask the program officer for a profile of the typical reviewer, like their age, education and experience.

Step 4 - Contact the Funder Representative

When you reach the contact person on the funder's staff you wish to speak with, say that you have studied their application and guidelines extensively and you have some questions. Ask if he or she has 10 minutes now or if you should schedule 10 minutes at a more convenient time. Briefly describe your project, its benefits and outcomes.

Here are 13 questions to ask the funder representative …

1. After hearing your description, does this idea fall within the current priorities?

2. Since the average award last year was $X,XXX, is this likely to change?

3. What's the current grant-making budget for this year?

4. How much will be given to continuation grants and how much will be given to new awards?

5. Are you planning to use a special criteria in selecting awards, such as a geographic area or type of organization?

6. Is yours one-time-only support or will it allow other funding opportunities?

7. What is the projected application-to-selection ratio?

8. What are the most commonly-made mistakes found in proposals that you received?

9. Have other applicants overlooked anything that you would like to see addressed in a proposal?

10. Would you be willing to review a pre-proposal concept paper of 2 or 3 pages?

11. Do you have a previously-funded proposal that you recommend that we take a look at as one that you think is 'good' in terms of the format and style that you prefer?

12. How are proposals reviewed? Who are the reviewers?

13. Would you be willing to provide us with a copy of the evaluation form and rating scale that reviewers use?

In addition to asking questions, be prepared to answer questions that they may have for you like the 7 questions below:

1. What's unique about your proposal?

2. What new information will your project tell us?

3. Is this an area that is already heavily funded?

4. What kind of difference will your project make?

5. What's timely about your project?

6. How will you disseminate the results of your project?

7. What kind of impact will your project have beyond the narrow geographic focus that you serve?

In review, making a pre-proposal contact with a funder will increase your chances of being approved threefold. Pre-proposal contacts serve three primary purposes …

1. To verify the information

2. To gather more information

3. To make a positive first impression

The 4 steps in the pre-proposal contact process are …

1. Ask for application forms and guidelines

2. Contact a past grantee

3. Contact a prior reviewer

4. Contact the funder representative

This concludes Secret 21. In the next secret, you'll discover how to save time in your grant proposal writing knowing what to look for in application forms and guidelines.

Secret 22 – Save Time By Scanning The Application Forms And Guidelines

From the funder research that you've done already and from your pre-proposal contact, you should be able to identify the application forms, guidelines, and specifications for each funder to whom you are submitting a grant proposal.

Funders often do have their own guidelines they would like applicants to follow. These are designed to gather efficiently the information the particular funder wants to use in determining which proposals to fund.

Government sources often call their guidelines "Requests for Proposals" or RFP's. Sometimes, they refer to them as "Requests for Applications" - RFA's.

15 Items to Look For in an RFP

Here are 15 items to scan for when you analyze an RFA or RFP …

1. Deadline

2. Eligibility

3. Required forms

4. Required signatures

5. Recipient type; that is, the type of agency the funder would like to fund

6. Any measurable outcomes that the funder expects from you

7. Criteria used for evaluating proposals

8. Time span for your project, like 1 year or 5 years

9. Total amount of funding per grant

10. Geographic area of focus

11. Population to be served

12. Any required 'support' documents, such as staff resumes, your agency's annual budget, the IRS determination letter, your agency's mission

statement, any letters of support or letters of endorsement, formulas for calculating staff benefits, and indirect costs calculations

13. Any special budget requirements, such as following guidelines set by the U.S. Office of Management and Budget, which are referred to as OMB circulars – Office of Management and Budget.

14. Technical assistance workshops, if they are provided

15. Name and contact information for the funder representative or official

2 Common Reasons for Being Rejected

The 2 most commonly cited reasons for rejecting proposals are:

1. The proposal was submitted too late. The deadline was missed.

2. Instructions weren't followed.

Just by paying attention to the deadline and following instructions, you can increase the possibility of your project getting funded.

The grant proposal writing experts provide another tip. They say, "Notice the headings and subheadings in the RFP and in the evaluation form, if you get one. If the RFP or evaluation has a sub-heading called "Administration," you should put a sub-heading in your proposal called "Administration." Avoid being overly creative and calling it "Staff" or "Project Management." This isn't rocket science. Just use the same headings and subheadings that the funder uses in the RFP and evaluation form.

Remember to look for information from government grants on technical assistance workshops. These will acquaint you with funder procedures and guidelines, as well as the elements they are looking for in a successful proposal.

Your funder research should also provide you with information about the decision on how proposals will be approved or rejected. Your research should include the review process, the physical location, the time allowed for each proposal, as well as a profile of who will be reviewing the proposals, information on who is making the final decision, and even a copy of the evaluation form that is used by the funders.

Later, once you've drafted your proposal, these materials will come in handy when others critique your grant before you submit it.

Finally, having done your due diligence in funder research, including a pre-proposal contact with a funder, you are in a position to determine if there is indeed a match between your project and the funder's priorities.

The result should be a 'yes' or 'no' answer to this question, "Is there a good match between the funder and my agency?" If your idea matches the priorities and interests of a funder, as well as fits the funder's funding timeline, then move on to customizing your proposal. If 'not', cut your losses and don't waste more of your time or a funder's.

In review, you can save time and headaches by learning how to scan application forms and guidelines. Government grants often refer to these as Requests for Proposal (RFP's) or Requests for Application (RFA's). This Secret includes 15 items for you to look for in an RFP.

This concludes Secret 22. This also concludes the section on 2nd step of the grant proposal writing process: what we call "researching funders."

Once you research and find a funder and get a 'yes' to a good match between the funder and your agency, you are indeed ready to customize your proposal to the funder specifications. The next six secrets focus on how you can tailor your proposal.

In the next secret, we'll focus on how to create a timeline for success.

STEP 3
CUSTOMIZE
YOUR PROPOSAL

Secret 23 – Create A Timeline For Success

"I can teach anybody how to get what they want out of life.
The problem is that I can't find anyone who can tell me what they want."

-Mark Twain

Secret 23 is the first of 6 secrets in Step 3 of the grant proposal writing process: Customize Your Proposal.

100% of the top grant proposal writing experts agree that it is important to customize your proposal to funder specifications. This Secret will show you how to do that including ways to make your proposal stand out.

Let's assume that you have a draft of the plan for your idea in one hand and a potential funder's application and guidelines in the other. You're ready to customize your proposal to meet the funder's specifications.

Customizing your proposal will help you complete your first draft and get your draft reviewed. The more specific and concise the feedback you can get from others, the better able you will be to revise the first draft so it aligns closely with what funders are looking for.

Let's spend a little time getting organized so that we can put together a winning proposal.

Create A Timeline

Let's create a timeline.

For every grant proposal I write, I establish a timeline to put together the proposal. I begin by working backwards from the final deadline. So, let's take a piece of paper. Draw an "X" on the left side of the paper and another "X" on the right side. Then, connect the two "X's" by drawing a straight line.

Above the "X" on the left side, write *"Today's Date."* Above the "X" on the right side, write *"Deadline."* This is your timeline.

We want to identify the specific tasks that have to be completed prior to sending off the proposal. I establish a deadline for completing each of the 7 tasks that I'm about to mention. My goal is to give myself ample time to complete them so I'm not overly stressed at the end.

The deadlines I set for myself make up the grant timeline.

So, we've got *today's date* and the final *deadline* on our timeline. These are the two end points. I like to move backwards along the line, starting with the end in sight.

Ideally, I want to have my proposals arrive 14 days - that only 10 working days - prior to the deadline. Why? If mine is a new agency applying for funds, this will leave a good first impression. An early submission gives the impression that you will get your reports in on time and that you're organized. Plus, you want to avoid the last-minute rush and get stockpiled with any last-minute submissions.

Now, put an "X" on your timeline 2 weeks before the *deadline*. Write "*Submission*" above your "X". If you have the actual deadline date of your grant, then put the actual date. So, if your grant *deadline* is *March 31*, then write this down as your *deadline*. Then, your 14-day *submission* date would be *March 17*.

Create A Timeline

January 15	March 17	March 31
_____	_____	_____
Today's Date	*Submission*	*Deadline*

X--X--------------------X

Keep in mind that if there are others on the grant proposal writing team, make sure to share the timeline and the tasks with them so that you're all "on the same page." This helps with delegating tasks, too. But, I'm getting ahead of myself.

Next, I like to figure out who the individuals are who need to sign the application. In other words, whose signatures are required on the final version of the proposal? This is very important because Murphy's Law says that when you want to get your signatures, that'll be the time when the person is on vacation. So, I give myself a few days before the submission to get the required signatures.

How do I do this?

I call the person's office and ask the secretary for the person's schedule. I ask how much time that person will need to review the proposal before signing it. Then, I schedule a meeting to explain the grant. I give them time to review it. Then, I schedule a final meeting to come and pick it up. I don't rely on the mail system or the flow of paperwork. I walk my proposal through the process. I hand deliver it to the right people.

7 Steps To Customizing Your Proposal

Let's take a look at the 7 steps to customize your proposal to funder specifications:

Step 1 - Read through the funder guidelines several times to become familiar with the funder's specifications. Identify the deadlines, the forms to be completed, and any requirements, guidelines or suggestions. Highlight the key items.

Step 2 - Create a table of contents for your proposal. Use the headings and subheadings provided in the funder's guidelines and evaluation form, if it's available. Including the headings and subheadings that the funder uses makes it easier for the funder's own evaluators later to locate information quickly. If no headings or subheadings are provided by the funder, go ahead and create your own.

Step 3 - Write a first draft of your proposal. Keep in mind Secrets 6-13 that will show you how to make your project original, timely, problem-solving and compelling. Take a look at the sustainability plan ideas, as well as how to create your community needs assessment and the 8 basic sections of a winning proposal.

Step 4 - Conduct a mock review of the first draft using colleagues, friends, or family. Ask for feedback according to funder's decision-making process; that is, how they will ultimately rate your proposal. You'll get more information on the Mock Review process in Secret 28.

Step 5 - Revise the first draft based on the feedback you get from your mock review team.

Step 6 - Obtain any required agency signatures and letters of support.

Step 7 - Submit your proposal ideally 10 working days prior to the deadline.

I can't overstress the importance of tailoring your proposal to the expectations of a prospective funder. That's why creating a timeline will help you accomplish this. This small organizational tip can save you lots of headaches and rushing around at the last minute. And, if you're like me, when you are rushing around, something always falls through the cracks.

In review, create a timeline on a piece of paper with *today's date* on the left and the *deadline* on the right. Count back 14 days. That's your early *submission* date. Then, contact the office of the individuals whose signatures you need. Find out when they're available and the preferred time that they need to review and sign it. Walk your proposal through the bureaucracy.

There are 7 steps to customizing your proposal to the funder specifications:

1. Step 1 - Read through the funder guidelines several times.

2. Step 2 - Create a table of contents using the headings and subheadings provided in the funder.

3. Step 3 - Write a first draft.

4. Step 4 - Conduct a mock review of your first draft.

5. Step 5 - Revise the first draft based on the feedback from your mock review team.

6. Step 6 - Obtain any required agency signatures and letters of support.

7. Step 7 - Submit your proposal ideally 14 days or 10 working days prior to the deadline.

    This concludes Secret 23.

    In the next secret, we'll explore the best attitude for us to adopt while we're putting together a winning proposal.

Secret 24 – Adopt The Right Winning Attitude

"If you think you can do a thing or think you can't do a thing, you're right."

-Henry Ford

On my fortieth birthday, some friends of mine threw a party for me at a local restaurant. At the party, my friends shared what they appreciated about me. One of the employees from the restaurant must have been listening. He had taken some university classes with me. As we walked out of the restaurant, he said, "You know, Phil, what I've appreciated about you since I've known you for 15 years now is your 'winning attitude.' In fact, you have a Joe Montana winning attitude."

The attitude you bring to your grant proposal writing can make or break your proposal, as well as determine whether you're going to have fun in the process. If you want to have fun, adopt a winning attitude right from the start. That's what Secret 24 is all about.

7 Top Winning Attitudes

Winning Attitude 1 - Build Relationships & Develop Partnerships - There are several key relationships and partnerships to keep in mind.

First, there's the relationship between your agency and the donor. Your agency has the ideas and capacity to solve problems but no money to implement your ideas. The foundations, corporations and government agencies have money but not the resources to make it happen. Bringing the two of you together results in a dynamic collaboration.

Keep in mind that there are key people and community agencies for you to partner with. Partnerships allow for shared resources and mutual benefit. When people and agencies do what they do best and delegate the rest, we all benefit - and have more fun in the process. We can all do more collectively that any of us can do individually. Plus we all can grow and enjoy ourselves more when we do what we do best and delegate the rest.

Winning Attitude 2 - Employ A Win-Win-Win Attitude - Imagine that you can get your personal needs met. Imagine that your agency can get its needs met. Imagine now that a funding source and your community and even your clients can get all of their needs met, all at the same time. It's a win-win-win-win situation. Or, at least it could be, if you allow it to happen with a win-win attitude.

Imagine partnerships with other agencies where all are winners. Your clients win, funders win - everyone wins!

Winning Attitude 3 - Invite Investment - Invite a potential donor to invest in your idea and organization by giving you a grant. Remember that everyone likes to be on the side of a winner. Sound like a winner from the start, and invite investments into your plan. Money is sure to follow.

Winning Attitude 4 – Build Credibility First - Funders want to ensure that their money is going to be spent wisely and appropriately. They want to know that the applying agency has a track record of success.

When they look at proposals submitted for funding, they will likely review the credibility of your agency, giving more points to those agencies with credibility.

A fundraiser recently told me, "In my experience, the number one tip to fundraising millions is to have credibility."

If your agency is just starting out or has poor credibility, you need to develop its credibility by trying some of the following strategies:

- Partner with an agency that does have credibility,

- Create the image of where your agency is headed,

- Strengthen the advisory board,

- Include the names of your credible board members on your agency's stationery.

Winning Attitude 5 - Be Brief and Concise - One grant proposal writing expert put it this way:

Winning Attitude 6 - Focus On The Clients' Needs First - We talked about this in Secret 12 when we talked about assessing the needs of your community first. So, write from that perspective. It's the needs of the clients who will benefit from the funded project, the needs of community and the needs of the funder. Focus on their needs rather than your needs first.

Winning Attitude 7 - Focus On Sustainability Up Front - I learned this lesson the hard way. When $2.5 million in federal grant funding ran out after five years, there was no way to keep the language learning program open. I had to let go of 25 teachers and tell 3,000 students that they no longer had classes.

We were able to sustain some classes on a fee-for-service basis. However, the heart of the program died with the funding. I hadn't realized until it was too late that getting the funding as "seed money" is only the first step. Sustaining your program after initial funding requires additional planning up front. That's why I included the 21 strategies for a killer sustainability plan. It's in Secret 10. I don't want you to go through what I had to.

Bonus Winning Attitude 8 - Volunteer To Evaluate Proposals – You can gain valuable experience by becoming a volunteer grant reviewer. When you actually review proposals in a real review process, you learn a great deal about how funding decisions are made, as well as have the opportunity to read well-written proposals as well as poorly-written proposals. Volunteer for a government agency, such as city, county and state government, as well as a foundation or corporation that you know about.

In review, there are 7 winning attitudes and 1 bonus attitude that you can use to have more fun and increase your chances of success …

1. Build Relationships & Develop Partnerships

2. Employ A Win-Win-Win Attitude

3. Invite Investment

4. Build Credibility First

5. Be Brief And Concise

6. Focus On The Clients' Needs First

7. Focus On Sustainability Up Front

8. BONUS - Volunteer To Evaluate Proposals

Adopting one or more of these 8 winning attitudes, and it will increase your success rate dramatically. This concludes Secret 24. Next time, we'll focus on assembling the support data that we need as we move through the grant proposal writing process.

Secret 25 – Assemble Support Data

To help prove that there's a problem or need in your community and to refine your approach to addressing a need, it's important to have some sort of statistical data to support yourself. Many beginning grant writers make sweeping, unsupported statements in their needs statement section of their proposals, yet these prove to be assumptions that lack adequate statistical backup and validation. What this means is that you need to have statistical support for your argument.

Good sources for statistical data include …

- Your local or state reference library,

- The U.S. Census Bureau website,

- Professional journals,

- Professional associations,

- Reports from commissions or government offices citing pertinent needs,

- Special reports,

- News magazines, and

- Newspapers.

Also, most funders will request that you have support material to include in the appendix of your proposal.

Here's a tip: start collecting the support data and support material you need for your appendix early on in the process. I like to create a folder where I can put in support data as it comes across my desk and computer screen. Gathering this support data when you think about it and collecting important pieces as you go leaves you with less things to worry about at the last minute, when your stress levels are higher.

Here's a list of 24 support data items that you can start collecting right away:

1. Your agency's IRS determination letter

2. Resumes of staff

3. Letters of support from other community agencies (They are also called letters of recommendation, letters of endorsement, or letters of commitment.)

4. Job descriptions of project staff funded by the proposal

5. Your activity timeline

6. A budget narrative

7. Your sustainability plan

8. Your evaluation plan

9. Evidence of previous success, as in newspaper articles and reports

10. Summaries of previous fiscal audits

11. Test or statistical data

12. List of agencies in your consortium, coalition or network

13. Glossary of terms

14. Footnotes or endnotes

15. Your DUNS number, which stands for "Dun and Bradstreet"

16. Overall budget summary of previous year or three years

17. Newsletters, annual reports or brochures

18. Your strategic plan

19. Your needs assessment

20. Tables, charts or graphics illustrating your problem or your successes

21. Minutes of advisory committee meetings

22. Architect's drawings

23. Other agency publications

24. List of funders you plan to approach for support

In review, in order to support your claims and assumptions, find statistical support for your argument. Two good sources for statistical data are your local library and the U.S. Census Bureau website.

A smart tip is to start collecting support material for your appendix early on in the process. You never know what the funder is going to ask for, but at least you'll be prepared. Two types of support documents to collect right away are your IRS determination letter and your Duns and Bradstreet number.

This concludes Secret 25. Next time, we'll look at world-class writing tips to make your proposal stand out.

Secret 26 – Use 14 World-Class Writing Tips

A clear, concise style of writing can go a long way in making your proposal stand out. In this Secret, you'll learn 14 world-class writing tips from the experts:

1. Shorter words are better than long, complex ones.

2. Separate paragraphs with a space. Putting in paragraphs breaks up the body copy and helps the eyes flow down the page.

3. Use simple sentences of no more than 2 commas.

4. Use short paragraphs of no more than 5 to 7 lines per paragraph.

5. Use your computer's spell checker, grammar checker, and thesaurus.

6. Define all acronyms the first time you show them. For example, for College of Southern Nevada (CSN), put (CSN) in parenthesis.

7. Avoid first-person writing. Use 'they' or 'them' instead of "she/he" or 'his' or 'her'.

8. Support all your assumptions with statistics or statements from authorities.

9. Watch out for tentative and iffy statements, like 'may' and 'might'. Be as positive and confident as you can be. Use 'can' and 'will' instead.

10. Use transitional phrases. These are words that signal connection and coherence between paragraphs. These signal to the reader how one idea is connected to another. Here are 12 examples: to illustrate, to contrast, to add, to relate in time, to related in space, to create a similarity, to show emphasis, to provide details, to include an example, to show a consequence or result, to make a suggestion, and to summarize.

Checklist - Transitional Phrases

☐ To *illustrate*, use … thus, for example, for instance, namely, to illustrate, in other words, in particular, specifically, such as

☐ To *contrast*, use … on the contrary, contrarily, notwithstanding, but, however, nevertheless, in spite of, in contrast, yet, on one hand, on the other hand, rather, or, nor, conversely, at the same time, while this may be true

- ☐ To *add*, use … and, in addition to, furthermore, moreover, besides, than, too, also, both-and, another, equally important, first, second, etc., again, further, last, finally, not only-but also, as well as, in the second place, next, likewise, similarly, in fact, as a result, consequently, in the same way, for example, for instance, however, thus, therefore, otherwise

- ☐ To relate in *time*, use … after, afterward, before, then, once, next, last, at last, at length, first, second, etc., at first, formerly, rarely, usually, another, finally, soon, meanwhile, at the same time, for a minute, hour, day, etc., during the morning, day, week, etc., most important, later, ordinarily, to begin with, afterwards, generally, in order to, subsequently, previously, in the meantime, immediately, eventually, concurrently, simultaneously

- ☐ To relate in *space*, use … at the left, at the right, in the center, on the side, along the edge, on top, below, beneath, under, around, above, over, straight ahead, at the top, at the bottom, surrounding, opposite, at the rear, at the front, in front of, beside, behind, next to, nearby, in the distance, beyond, in the forefront, in the foreground, within sight, out of sight, across, under, nearer, adjacent, in the background

- ☐ To create a *similarity*, use … similarly, likewise, in like fashion, in like manner, analogous to

- ☐ To show *emphasis*, use … above all, indeed, truly, of course, certainly, surely, in fact, really, in truth, again, besides, also, furthermore, in addition

Checklist - More Transitional Phrases

- ☐ To provide *details*, use … specifically, especially, in particular, to explain, to list, to enumerate, in detail, namely, including

- ☐ To include an *example*, use … for example, for instance, to illustrate, thus, in other words, as an illustration, in particular

- ☐ To show a *consequence* or *result*, use … so that, with the result that, thus, consequently, hence, accordingly, for this reason, therefore, so, because, since, due to, as a result, in other words, then

- ☐ To make a *suggestion*, use … for this purpose, to this end, with this in mind, with this purpose in mind, therefore

- ☐ To *summarize*, use … therefore, finally, consequently, thus, in short, in conclusion, in brief, as a result, accordingly

11. Avoid using ALL CAPITAL LETTERS in titles and headings. Instead, use Upper And Lower-Case Letters.

12. Highlight the main points of your arguments and proposal. Use bold, italics, tabs or indents, and bullet and number lists.

13. To make the proposal less formal and easier to read, use ellipses dots (...) and also parenthetical dashes (-). This makes the proposal more conversational, as if one person is talking to another.

14. Instead of writing long paragraphs of narrative, use "bulleted or numbered lists." Cluster your lists into groups of 3-7 items. The best uses of lists are to indicate:

    - A sequence

    - Steps in a process

    - Parts or materials needed

    - Important items to remember

    - Specific criteria

    - Key recommendations

    - Conclusions

In review, in this Secret we covered 14 world-class writing tips, such as ways to make your writing more conversational, adding transitional phrases, and adding bullets and numbers lists.

This concludes Secret 26. In the next secret, we'll discuss top ways to dress up your proposal and make it stand out.

Secret 27 – Dress Up Your Proposal

The layout of your proposal - how it appears on the page - contributes a lot to its readability. When yours is among many proposals that a reviewer must read, a good-looking, clear, yet simple layout and presentation will make a good impression and help the reviewer access the information quickly.

Grant writing is a competitive process. Sponsors receive many ideas. You could have a very good idea, but so will others. When many good proposals are submitted, often it's the secondary factors that influence the final decision. One such factor is your proposal's appearance.

9 Ways to Dress Up Your Proposal

Here are 9 suggestions from the experts on how to improve the appearance of your proposal:

1. Use headings and subheadings used by the funder in the guidelines and evaluation form. Use headings and subheadings even in letter proposals. Headlines spaced within the body copy can make the document more readable.

2. Use specific numbers in titles and headings. For example, "9 Ways to Dress Up Your Proposal" is more specific than "Ways to Dress Up Your Proposal." For some reason, readers are intrigued by numbers in titles.

3. Use the font style used by funders in their publications whenever possible. If you cannot find a funder font, consider using what's called a serif font – I'll explain that in a moment - for the text because it is easier for the eyes to follow for long narratives. Use the type called sans serif for titles and headings. Let me explain …

   - For text … Serif fonts are those with little strokes on the end, like:

     Times Roman
     Courier
     Garamond

- For titles and headings … San serif fonts are the ones without the small finishing strokes at the end, like:

  Arial
  Tahoma
  Verdana

4. Leave ample white space. Using white space can break up long text. Some top experts suggest that you dedicate about 50 percent of each page to white space. One way to add space is to double-space between minor sections and triple-space between major sections. Also, keep your paragraphs short - to 5-7 lines.

5. Justify the left margin. But, leave the right margin 'unjustified'.

6. Use blue ink when signing all original forms, unless otherwise directed. In this way, the originals will stand out from the photocopies.

7. Put short illustrations, charts and other tables into your narrative so the reader doesn't have to go back-and-forth between the narrative and appendix to find them.

8. Include an activity timeline. Most grant proposals are written primarily in narrative form. An occasional table and chart can break up long text and provide a visual method for delivering information. Grant activities, designed to reach your program goals and objectives, can be presented in a table format with the activities in the left-most column. Months or dates for completion can be included as additional columns to the right. Then, for each activity a check mark can be made in the column of the months in which the activity will be completed. See your sample activity timeline table (*below*).

ACTIVITY TIMELINE

ACTIVITY	11/98	12/98	1/99	2/99	3/99	4/99	5/99	6/99	7/99	8/99	9/99	10/99	11/99	12/99
Secure a web address and link current web-page	X													
Secure electronic mailing list and regular mailing list for individuals and agencies	X	X												
Design and print flyers	X	X												
E-mail electronic flyer			X											
Mail three-fold flyer			X											
Purchase qeuipment for interviews/audio clips	X													
Conduct, record, and edit interviews/audio clips		X	X	X	X	X	X							
Hire web consultant to put audio clips and transcripted versions on the website							X	X						
Evaluate outcomes and processes														X

9. Include a budget narrative. Most budgets are written in spreadsheet format. However, many items in a budget are often left out of the proposal's main narrative. The problem and the methods of addressing it are usually explained clearly in the narrative, but a detailed explanation of which funds will be used for what is usually lacking. Therefore, I find it helpful to include a brief explanation of 1-2 sentences for each budgeted expense and then relate it to the overall grant.

In review, in this Secret you learned 9 ways to make your proposal stand out from the competition, such as using the font style of the funder, leaving the right margin unjustified, and including an activity timeline and budget narrative.

This concludes Secret 27. In the next secret, you'll discover how to triple your chances of being funded by conducting a mock review of your first draft.

Secret 28 – Triple Your Chances With Mock Reviews

Once you have a first draft of your proposal, it's a great idea to conduct a mock review. Unfortunately, most grant writers didn't get the memo. They submit proposals that are no more than first drafts, sent in un-reviewed.

Think about it for a minute. If what you're turning in is essentially a first draft, the actual reviewers are the ones who find things that are missing in the first go-around. That won't set you apart from the competition. In fact, that's a huge liability for you. It decreases the likelihood of being funded by 200%.

However, if you can create an image in your mind of what the review process will ultimately be like for the funder and then recreate a mock review team that basically mirrors that review process; you'll discover any mechanical errors and get valuable feedback to help you improve the clarity of the proposal from the eyes of the reviewers. That's key … improving your grant from the eyes of the reviewers … wow! Imagine that!

I've been teaching the mock review feedback loop for many years as a way to double your chances of getting funded. Then, I researched the grant experts and found that most of them were saying that their mock reviews actually tripled their chances of being funded. Double or triple … what's most important is that you create a review team like the one that will ultimately pass judgment on your proposal. This will increase your chances of success.

In your pre-proposal contact, you did your best to get a list of the funder's reviewers for the previous year, as well as the scoring system that will be used. If you didn't get a list of previous reviewers, then create a composite profile of the average reviewer.

For example, for one grant, I found out that the readers were 90% from the business world and 10% were educators. I learned that many of the readers liked to see the following "buzz words" addressed in the proposal: "accountability," "business involvement in planning and implementation," "sustainability after the funding is gone," and "partnerships." I also found out that I should avoid using 'teacherese' – those are the technical words like "competency-based instruction" or "Bloom's Taxonomy" – that meant nothing to the evaluators. In other words, don't use jargon!

If you are not able to get a list of reviewers or create a profile, consider that the majority of proposal readers are....

- Republicans

- Affluent or rich

- Educated

- Golfers rather than bowlers

- Male

- Middle aged or older

- Conservative

- Members of the ethnic majority group

- Hard-working

- Business people

- Legalistic

- Capitalists, not socialists

Think about your audience when you are writing your proposal. Think about your mock review team.

Here are 8 pieces of information to provide them ...

1. Reviewer profile - Who is your reviewer?

2. Training - How much training do reviewers get?

3. Setting – In what setting will the review take place? ... At the agency's office? ... At the reviewer's home? Or, at both sites?

4. Review process - Is there any discussion about the proposals after they're reviewed? Does one defend while others try to find flaws?

5. Evaluation form - What form will the reviewers use to evaluate your proposals?

6. Scoring system - What scoring system will be used?

7. Selection criteria - How will the top proposals be chosen? Will they be chosen based on the highest scores – for example, only proposals scoring about 97 will be considered? What selection criteria will be used?

8. Time spent – How much time is spent on an average per proposal?

5 Steps of Your Mock Review Process

Here are 5 steps of the Mock Review process …

Step 1 - Complete a Worksheet for conducting a mock proposal review (*on Page 141*). This form includes the information collected during your pre-proposal contact and from the funder's guidelines and specifications. Here is what you'll need for your worksheet …

1. Name of funder

2. Your name

3. Description of the funder

4. Funder preferences and requirements. If possible, bring copies of application and guidelines.

5. Profile the reviewer(s) in as much detail as possible

6. Describe the rating criteria. Bring copies of funder evaluation form or use the Generic Evaluation Form that's provided to you (*on Page 142*).

7. Describe how proposals would be selected for approval and who will make the final decision

8. Describe the review process.

Step 2 - Identify colleagues or friends who will be interested in participating. It is helpful to explain up front the overall process and reason for conducting a mock review and how important their feedback is to you in improving your proposal.

Most participants comment afterwards that the mock review process is an interesting experience; they learn a great deal about grant proposal writing and about your idea in the process. They usually greatly appreciate being asked and welcome the opportunity to be part of a process that will help get you closer to getting funded.

To entice them to participate, bribing helps. You may wish to buy them lunch and/or give them some sort of gift, as well as schedule the review around the times and dates that are convenient for them.

Step 3 - Conduct the mock review. Make sure to follow as closely as possible the actual review process that the funder uses. The worksheet will provide the review team with enough information to take on the role of the actual funder review team.

The tendency for new grant writers is to trivialize this experience and not follow exactly what the funder's review process is; instead, they might ask for general feedback. While this is helpful, it will not yield the very specific funder information that a mock review process can provide - feedback that will help you take your draft to the next level.

Step 4 – Listen. It's important to set your ego aside and listen open-heartedly to the feedback from the review team. Harsh comments are often hard to digest. However, sometimes these are the very comments that you need to let in the most. They will improve your proposals the most. Comments - whether harsh or complementary - when received with an open mind of curiosity and wonder – will help you improve the proposal.

Remember that you want accurate feedback that reflects what an actual funder review team might be thinking.

Step 5 - Edit Your Proposal and Submit It. Incorporating the feedback from the mock review process, do a final edit of your proposal, or ask a friend or colleague to do the edit. Then put together the entire proposal, and secure all the required signatures.

Double check to make sure all the forms, additional copies, supplementary materials and your appendixes are included. There should be a table of contents, and the pages should be numbered consecutively. Submit your proposal approximately 14 days – or 10 working days - before the deadline. One group of authors suggested that you plan it so your proposal arrives in the middle of the week - on a Tuesday or Wednesday. Most agencies receive less mail on these two days, so your proposal will get more notice.

In review, a mock review of your proposal will double even triple your chances of being funded. The 8 pieces of information to provide to your mock review team are the reviewer profile, training they get, setting, the review process, evaluation form, the scoring system, selection criteria, and the time spent per proposal.

There are 5 steps to the mock review process …

Step 1 - Complete the Worksheet for conducting a mock review (*page 141*).

Step 2 - Identify colleagues or friends who would be interested in participating.

Step 3 - Conduct the mock review.

Step 4 – Listen.

Step 5 - Edit Your Proposal And Submit It.

This concludes Secret 28, as well as all the secrets related to Step 3 – Customize Your Proposal. In the next section, we will discuss Step 4 – Respond to the Funder's Decision - and how to celebrate or transform failure into success.

Worksheet - Mock Review

Name of potential funder _____

Name of grant writer _____

Describe potential funder _____

_____

_____

Funder preferences and requirements (bring copies of application/guidelines)

_____

_____

Profile your reviewer(s) in as much detail as possible

_____

_____

Describe rating criteria (Bring copies of funder form or design and bring your own. If funder has rating form, use it. If not, create your own.)

_____

_____

Describe how proposals will be selected for approval and who will make final decision

_____

_____

Describe review process:

How much time does each reviewer have with each proposal?_____

Describe the location where the review will take place _____

Proposal Evaluation Form (Generic)

Proposal Title_____   Date_____

12 Key Components	1 = poor 5 = excellent		Comments
Does the outline (format) of the proposal match the format required by the funding source?	Yes	No	
The proposal has few, if any, unsupported assumptions.	1 2 3 4 5		
The proposal includes quotes from authority figures or clients and/or statistical evidence to support assumptions and statements.	1 2 3 4 5		
The proposal is neat, clean, and easy to read.	1 2 3 4 5		
The proposal is brief, clear, and concise.	1 2 3 4 5		
The proposal is positive.	1 2 3 4 5		
The proposal has a professional look and layout.	1 2 3 4 5		
The proposal establishes the credibility of the applicant.	1 2 3 4 5		
The program objectives are measurable outcomes.	1 2 3 4 5		
The proposal includes a timeline for program activities.	1 2 3 4 5		

The budget includes detailed information and matches the objectives.	1 2 3 4 5	
What is your overall evaluation of the proposal?	1 2 3 4 5	

What are the strengths of the proposal?

What are the weaknesses of the proposal?

What additional information would you like to have as a reader?

_____   _____

Evaluator's Signature   Date

STEP 4
RESPOND TO
THE DECISION

Secret 29 – Celebrate! Or, Transform Your Failure Into Success

This Secret is the only one that focuses on Step 4 of the grant proposal writing process, namely "Respond To The Funder's Decision." In this Secret, you'll learn the importance of responding to the funder's decision, and if needed how to reframe a rejection into a success.

Unless you have the opportunity for an oral presentation or defense of your proposal, once your proposal has been submitted, there's really nothing to do but wait. At some point, you will be informed of the funder's decision.

Whether you get funded or not, you should always respond to the decision in the best possible way. It is helpful to think that it may take you three times to get the funding you want. Knowing this lets you reframe a rejection into a positive experience that might just help you become successful.

If you are turned down, you can ask for feedback about why you were turned down. In addition, you can ask if the funder might still be interested in your idea, and if they think you should re-apply. If the funder says 'no', most likely your idea didn't match theirs to begin with. However, if the funder says 'yes' and encourages you to re-apply, ask for feedback that can help you bring your proposal more in line with what the funder is looking for.

Believe it or not, funders are on your side. They want to fund good proposals. So if your idea is something that they would be glad to reconsider, they will help you improve your proposal.

Pay attention because this is the closest thing to a guarantee in winning grants that you'll ever hear ...

What I'm about to share with you actually happened. A funder and I had this conversation walking into a building at California State (University) Sacramento. The funder was an Arts Council selection committee member.

She asked me this question: "Why do you think that the majority of people who are denied in their first try seldom, if ever, apply a second time?"

"Well, that's a good question," I replied. "My best guess is …
- That the applicants never realize that re-applying is even an option,
- They take rejection personally, and
- They never find out why they were denied and how to improve their proposals."

120

She said, "Yes, you're probably right. The interesting thing is that if applicants ask for feedback, we would give it to them. Then, if they revise their grant proposals and submit them a second time, the chance we would fund them actually doubles."

Here's the truly amazing part...

She continued, "If an applicant is denied that second time, but asks for feedback, improves her proposal, and re-submits a revised grant proposal for a third time, I can pretty much guarantee you that that proposal will be funded."

"Wow!" I thought. Did you hear that?

It's not "1-2-3 strikes ... you're OUT" like in baseball. It's actually "1-2-3 strikes, and you're IN!" Guaranteed!

Now, that's a game changer.

No teacher, book, expert or mentor ever told me that!

Likewise, most applicants fail to develop a long-term and mutual beneficial relationship with the grantor after a failure. The best relationship is the one based on honesty and sincere concern for the funder's unique needs. For example, saying "thank you" is a crucial element to relationship-building.

Thus, whether your proposal is approved or not approved, you should write a thank you letter to the funding organization.

Approved

Let's take a look at 7 things you can do if your proposal is approved.

1. The first action to take is to write a letter of thanks. Even though your proposal was successful, it's a good idea to ask for feedback about how it could have been improved. This information can help you in future grant proposal writing endeavors.

2. Request a copy of the reviewers' comments. Although most funders do not comment on your proposal, it doesn't hurt to ask.

3. Ask what they liked best about your proposal and what could have been improved.

4. Begin taking the steps to set up a good working relationship with your funder. You can start by inviting the official to come visit your site and also adding their names and emails to your PR list.

5. Find out what requirements the funder has for grantees. For example, ask about deadlines for your reports.

6. For private funders, find out the payment procedure.

   Put a note on your calendar to notify the funder 1-2 years after they have funded you to let them know how successful you were and to thank them again.

7. Find a special way to celebrate your approval. Take a photo of you holding your approval letter (or Big Check). Take your grant proposal writing team to dinner. Celebrate!

Above all, keep in mind that you and your agency are entering into a partnership with your funder. You are expecting to receive regular funds from them. In return, they are expecting that you will use those funds responsibly and in the manner described in your proposal. They will very likely appreciate feedback from you and updates, even if they don't formally ask for it.

Tips As You Implement Your Grant

Here are 4 tips for implementing your grant once it's funded …

1. Follow the activity timeline that you provided in your proposal. It is a great guide to help you with implementation, and it's a good tool to get everybody else on the same page.

2. Mark on your calendar when reports are due. Unless otherwise told, I plan to provide quarterly reports. It's a good habit to get into. I include performance and outcome data, as well as highlights, clippings from media coverage, and samples of promotional materials.

3. Never take the money and run. Be a good steward and spend the money on only what you agreed to spend it on.

4. Stay in close contact with the funder. Keep this in mind: by awarding you the grant, your funder is expressing a committed interest in your project and your agency. So, what do you do if you have a problem? Contact the funder as soon as possible after you've identified that there is a problem with the grant or project. Don't be afraid to contact the funder with bad news early on. If there's a problem, there's a lot they can do to help.

Pending

By "pending," I mean that you have submitted a proposal and no decision has been made regarding its approval or rejection. You're still waiting. If your proposal is pending approval, what should you do?

Funders tell us two things:

1. If there's a change 'within' your organization, let them know.

2. If you receive other grants from other sources for the same project under consideration, let them know.

Not Approved

If your proposal is "not approved," make the most of it by learning how to make your proposal better.

Here are 4 steps you can take to get the most out of a rejection …

Step 1 - Send A "Thank You" Letter

This is one way to set yourself apart from your competition. Appreciate the funder for the time and effort in considering your proposal for funding. Remind them how important they are as a source of funding.

One grant writer did just this. He sent his thank you letter. He was surprised when he got a response from the funder that said there had been a mistake and that his project should have gotten funding.

Step 2 - Ask For Feedback

- Ask what you can do to improve your proposal. This happened to a friend recently. I had just told him about the importance of asking for feedback. After his rejection, he asked the funder for feedback. The funder representative actually sat down with him for an hour or so and gave him great, specific feedback.

- Ask for verbatim reviewer comments, if possible. These are more specific and useful than general summary comments.

In a recent study, when asked if their foundation or corporation provided feedback in writing on all proposals they received, the majority of funder representatives said 'Yes'.

Step 3 - Ask About Re-Applying

- Ask whether the funder thinks your idea is a good match for them. Ask if your proposal has a chance of approval if you submit it again.

One funder says, "There is an amazing drop-off rate when an initial grant submission gets rejected. We seldom hear from the agency again." Another funder adds, "Send a letter asking if you can reapply. We turn applications down for two reasons. Either we ran out of grant money or the agency or their project was not a high priority for us."

After the funder sat down with my friend and gave him specific feedback, my friend thought he might have to wait for the next year and the next funding cycle. That wasn't the case at all, though. He was told to reapply right away. And, you know what? Last time I saw him, he said that he had gotten the money.

Step 4 - Maintain Contact With The Funder

- If the funder does express possible interest in your proposal in the future, keep occasional contact with them. Keep them abreast of important changes in your agency that are relevant to the project you want funding for.

- Send them a photocopy of articles or any publicity with a note saying something like, "Thought you might not have seen this and might be interested." Invite them to get to know your agency better by inviting them to special events. Avoid the "You only love me at submission time" syndrome.

What If They Say 'No' to Re-Applying

- Be creative. Even if the funding source you applied to advises against resubmitting your proposal, they can still be of help. Ask them if they could suggest another funder who might be interested in your project.

  Here is some advice directly from funders themselves …

- Keep in mind that a turndown is never personal. Try to step back. Be objective. If you've got questions, call.

- Take initiative to follow up and ask why you weren't funded. Ask for feedback. Keep the channels of communication open. This is a great way to build a relationship and let them know your character.

- Funders understand that you are disappointed. Keep in mind, though, that funders have to make hard choices about whom they fund and whom they don't. Again, rejection is not personal.

- Avoid becoming hostile by writing the board chair or coming to see the CEO. This raises the tension level and gets in the way of constructive dialogue.

- If you're angry, talk about the issue, and get it out. Find a constructive way to deal with your anger. If you tell everyone in your community, chances are that it will get back to the funder indirectly. In other words, be professional and deal with your anger on your own.

In review, always - that's always - send a "thank you" card - whether you are approved or rejected. We covered how to implement a grant when it's approved, what do to when it's pending, and 4 steps to turn a rejection into success …

Step 1 - Send A Thank You Letter

Step 2 - Ask For Feedback

Step 3 - Ask About Re-Applying

Step 4 - Maintain Contact With The Funder

This concludes Secret 29 and Step 4 of the grant proposal writing process: Respond to Funder's Decision. In our last secret, we'll conclude with a story about my mom and her first grant. If my mom can do it, so can you!

Secret 30 – If My Mom Can Do It, So Can You!

Several years ago, I received a call from my mom, who lives in Michigan. She was bubbly and full of excitement. "You'll never guess what your mom did," she said. "I wrote and got a grant approved from the state to make some renovations to the day care."

You see, my mom runs a day care center, called Grandma's Day Care, out of her home, and she does it for at-risk inner city children.

"That's great, mom. Congratulations!" I was so surprised and so proud.

"We can finally fix up that drafty room in the south side of the house," she said. "And finally insulate it properly. And the state's going to pick up the tab. I bet you never though your old mom could get a grant."

Over the phone, I could tell she was beaming ear to ear.

Now, what's truly amazing about this is that my mother never once asked for my advice. She never asked me about grant proposal writing or how to put together a successful grant proposal. She went off, figured it out all by herself and likely poured in all of her heart and soul.

The result was that she got her very first grant funded … without her son's help.

So the moral of the story is . . .

After all is said and done - after 30 secrets - the most important things of what you've learned in these Secrets will stay with you. Forget what I told you. Forget what the experts have said. Pour all of your heart and soul into what you do. Rely on your skills, and trust your intuition. And if all else fails ... call my mom.

(Just kidding, mom. I know you're busy with the kids and dad.)

Next Step

Congratulations! You made it! I appreciate you reading and learning along with me over the last 30 secrets.

Before we discuss the next step, there is one piece of unfinished business. In some of the secrets, I referred to finding two particular grant proposal writing templates valuable. I'd like to give them to you right now.

The first template is *Program Planning & Proposal Writing* by Norton Kiritz. It's touted as the "most widely used grant proposal writing format in the world." It's a great template for longer proposals, like government grants.

The second template is *Program Planning & Writing* by Lynn Miner and Jeremy Miner. You'll find an excellent template for shorter 1-2 page letter proposals for private funders like foundations and corporations.

So, what's the next step?

1. Please leave a 5-star review on Amazon.com for this book. Remember that anything less than a 5-star review on Amazon is considered a failure. I wish this weren't the case, but it is! If you have any suggestions for improvement to make this a 5-star book in your mind, I would appreciate it if you contacted me directly (see #4 below) and let me know.

2. If you wish to receive an audio version of this book AND direct access to an instructor to ask questions, please sign up at **GrantWritingFastTrack.com**.

3. If you would like digital, 8 ½ x 11 versions of all checklists and worksheets in this book, visit **PhilJohncock.com/4-Steps**.

4. If you would like to connect with me, please go to **LinkedIn.com/in/PhilJohncock**.

5. I hope you consider becoming Grant Professional Certified (GPC). See next section for details.

I am honored that you have joined me on this journey. I hope our paths cross in the future. Until then, thank you for your time and interest!

Highest Regards,

Phil Johncock

Grant Professional Certification (GPC) Exam

According to the Grant Professionals Certification Institute (GPCI) website (GrantCredential.org), GPCI "administers the nationally recognized Grant Professional Certified (GPC) credential to grant professionals who meet eligibility requirements and successfully demonstrate proficiency in the required competencies.

The GPC certification is based on rigorous standards and ongoing research to meet real-world demands of grant professionals. GPC-credentialed grant professionals demonstrate excellence in the grants profession and, on average, report higher earnings than those without the credential."

The GPC Exam is designed for a *grant professional with three to five years of experience in the field within the past five years*.

WHY Is Grant Professional Certification (GPC) Important?

- Certification may provide for greater earnings potential. Many grant professionals who have become Grant Professional Certified (GPC) experience salary and wage increases based on their certification status. A 2009 salary study shows that on average GPC earns 7% more than their non-certified counterparts. In addition, GPC's are in high demand internationally.
- Certification can improve career opportunities and advancement. GPCI certification can give you the "edge" when being considered for a promotion or other career opportunities. GPCI certification clearly identifies you as an employee who has demonstrated mastery of grant proposal writing principles and techniques based on accepted best practices.
- Certification grants you more credibility. Certification from the Grant Professionals Certification Institute (GPCI) serves as an impartial, third-party endorsement of your knowledge and experience against international standards in the grant profession. It adds to your credibility as a grant writer and sets you apart from other professionals.
- Certification prepares you for greater on-the-job responsibilities. GPCI certification is a clear indicator of your willingness to invest in your own professional development. Certified professionals are aware of the

131

constantly changing environment around their profession and possess the desire to anticipate and respond to change.

- Certification improves skills and knowledge. Typically, achieving GPCI certification requires training, experience, study and "keeping up" with changes. GPCI certification showcases your individual mastery by confirming proficiency and knowledge in the field. GPCI certification also requires continual learning and demonstration of competency, proving you stay ahead of the curve in the grant profession.

- Certification demonstrates your commitment to the grant profession. Receiving GPCI certification shows your peers, supervisors and, in turn, funders like the federal government your commitment to your chosen career and your ability to perform to set standards such as post-award grant management.

- Certification enhances the profession's image. GPCI certification seeks to grow, promote and develop certified professionals, who can stand "out in front" as role models in the grant field.

- Certification reflects achievement. GPCI certification is a reflection of personal achievement because the individual has displayed mastery of his or her field by meeting requirements and standards set in the grant profession.

- Certification builds self-esteem. GPCI certification is a step toward defining yourself beyond a job description or academic degree while gaining a sense of personal satisfaction.

- Certification offers greater recognition from peers. As a Grant Professional Certified, you can expect increased recognition from your peers for taking that extra step in your professional career.

In this book, 40 sub-competencies and 8 of 9 competencies from the GPC Exam are addressed: For a complete list of GPC Exam competencies & sub-competencies addressed in this book, please download the list at **PhilJohncock.com/Go/4-Steps-GPC**.

About the Author

PHIL JOHNCOCK, M.A., M.MS. is an award-winning author, educator & consultant. He has written over 26 books including *Small Town, Big Problem: Solutions for Homelessness*.

Drawing from over 40 years as an innovative and award-winning author, educator and consultant to some of the U.S., Canadian & Mexican top corporations, along with his own experience in building virtual businesses – like the Alliance for Nevada Nonprofits -- from scratch, designing a 10-credit grant proposal writing certification program and a system for learning grant proposal writing that resulted in $1.2 Billion in funding in the first 2.5 years, Phil mentors with a "can do now" attitude and integrity!

An innovator in online education, Phil designed the first grant proposal writing class on the Internet in 1997.

For fun, Phil enjoys ecstatic dancing and making up impromptu celebratory songs on-the-spot while playing his acoustic guitar.

www.ingramcontent.com/pod-product-compliance
Lightning Source LLC
Chambersburg PA
CBHW081514220526
45467CB00010B/2907